See.
Life.
Different.

Joel Holm

ISBN: 0986181900
ISBN-13: 978-0-9861819-0-0

DEDICATION

This book is dedicated to the one Person who enables me to truly see life different: The Holy Spirit of God.

CONTENTS

ACKNOWLEDGMENTS

I thank my beautiful wife who correctly reminds me that different is not always truth. Thanks to Joy Neal who helped me convey these ideas clearly through writing. And finally a special thanks to the teachers, authors and thinkers who got me thinking.

Introduction

Throughout my travels in over ninety countries, one thing I've learned is that the basic, underlying stuff of life isn't that different no matter where you go. On the outside it may seem different. The food may taste different, the scenery may look different, and the lifestyle and cultural values may vary. But under it all are some basic things that are common to all of us.

Another thing we generally have in common is the tendency to form patterns, habits and mindsets—and then stick to them. Whether or not it's the best or the most true way to approach life, we get used to doing things a certain way or looking at things from the same angle. In doing so, we miss out on fresh ways to think and live.

A few of these "basic building blocks of life" (specifically, Christian life) have continually come up in my thinking, writing and teaching. This book is an exploration of seven of them: work, success, people, stuff, time, faith, and the future. I don't offer a broad, comprehensive breakdown of each area. But what I offer is a seed, an idea, or a perspective to consider. *What if we look at it like this?* Does that fit? Is it true? Would it work? Would it be better?

I would encourage you to approach this book as a series of seven pamphlets that can be engaged independently. Each chapter has an idea, and each idea has an actionable application for your life. Change happens one step at a time, and taking that next simple step is more important than having it all figured out from the beginning.

Like all of us who write about life and faith, I write as a pilgrim in the same journey. And like most of us who write about life and faith, I write for myself. After several decades of working through these ideas and perspectives, they still challenge some of my ways of thinking, and they still push me to see life different. I hope they'll do the same for you.

Joel Holm

Chapter One

Work

Serve wholeheartedly as if you were serving the Lord, not people.

Ephesians 6:7

All of us live our lives in boxes.

Most Christians have three main life compartments. The first is our God box, which we step into on Sunday mornings or whenever we're addressing what we call our "spiritual life." The second is our personal box, which includes our family time, recreation and social life. And finally we have our work box, where we live for about forty to sixty hours per week. (Or, if you're a stay-at-home parent to small children, about 168 hours per week.)

Compartmentalization is a useful and even a necessary mental tool. If you want to get anything done in life, you need to be able to set things aside and focus on the task at hand. The problem isn't that we compartmentalize; the problem is that God is one of our compartments. God doesn't want to be a box that we attend to at times. He wants to permeate every area of our lives.

The way we demolish our God box and invite Him into every area of our lives is to treat every act as an act of worship. Including my work? Especially our work! We see work as a necessary evil. Work is how we pay the bills and provide for our family. But if we had enough money, we would no longer keep our job. I was driving to work one day when I saw a billboard for the lottery. Some people may be able to pass a billboard for a twenty-eight million dollar jackpot without fantasizing about what it would be like to win it, but I cannot! I thought, "What's the first thing most people would do if they won the lottery?" Before going on vacations or donating to their favorite causes or buying luxury items, most people would quit their jobs.

But the Bible teaches that work is not a secular activity, nor a necessary evil. Work is an inherently spiritual activity, and by offering it as worship, we restore work it to its created purpose.

Hardwired to Worship

All of us were hardwired to worship, and therefore we *will* worship. If we're not worshipping the Lord, our worship will come out in other ways, directed at whatever else is most important to us. For some teenagers, that may be worshiping a pop star. For many of us, we may begin to worship our work. We can get so wrapped up in our occupation that we begin to idolize it, worship it, and even find our identity in it. What kind of worship do you think the work god demands? Work and more work, of course. The work god is an insatiable, demanding god.

Thank God it's Friday

So we can worship our work and use it as a way of shaping our identity and personal worth. We can dread our work and buy lottery tickets in hopes of escaping it. Maybe you idolize and worship your work, or maybe you feel exactly the opposite. But there is yet another approach to work—a life-giving approach—which we'll explore in the book of Ephesians.

Work as Worship

Before we jump into the jolting first part of Ephesians 6:5 -9, let's make sure we appropriately address the immediate issue.

God hates slavery. He abhors it. He hated it in our nation's history, he hates it today, and he hated it two thousand years ago when this chapter was written. When we read scripture, it's important to look not just at the acknowledgement of the sinful systems that were part of the societies and cultures of that day, but also at the ways God was challenging those systems and leading people further into his kingdom.

Paul's letter to the Ephesians, while "behind" where God has brought his people today, was at the time very progressive and counter-cultural. The fact that Paul addresses slaves in this letter means that slaves and free men were sitting in the same room, listening to his words. It means that he saw slaves as free moral agents and disciples of Christ. So while the matter of slavery in the Bible is a topic for other books entirely, we will draw five timeless truths from Paul's instructions to this workforce in his day.

> *Slaves, obey your earthly masters with respect and fear, and with sincerity of heart, just as you would obey Christ. Obey them not only to win their favor when their eye is on you, but as slaves of Christ, doing the will of God from your heart. Serve wholeheartedly as if you were serving the Lord, not people, because you know that the Lord will reward each one for whatever good they do, whether they are slave or free. And masters, treat your slaves in the same way. Do not threaten them, since you know that he who is both their Master and yours is in heaven, and there is no favoritism with him. (Eph. 6:5-9)*

These five verses have five important applications for our work as an act of worship.

Application One: If work is worship, then Christ is your true boss.

Verse five says that we should obey our earthly masters (bosses) just as we would obey Christ. If work is an act of worship, then Christ is our true boss.

This is a hard one to wrap our minds around. We see Christ as our Savior, our Healer, and our Counselor. Maybe he is the boss over our morals; maybe he is even the boss over our money. But Christ as our workplace boss? Doesn't Jesus have more spiritual things to do than oversee our time clocks and project deadlines?

I've actually never had a boss in the traditional sense. While I didn't set out to avoid having a boss, it just sort of happened that way. I worked my way through college as an entrepreneur, buying and selling. As a lead pastor, I was the boss over others. Since then I've been leading a ministry with a board of directors, but I am "the boss". So while I've had oversight, I've never found myself in a position of answering to one person about my day-to-day work activities.

When people hear that I've gone through most of my adult life without a boss, they often express jealousy. Our society values the idea of not having a boss. We like the idea of having total freedom over our time and decisions. But in truth, all of us who have decided to follow Jesus have a boss. I have a boss and you have a boss. Whether you work in cubicle for a large corporation or run an Internet-based company from your home, you have a boss.

If Christ is our boss, than our work must have some kind of significance, right? Why would Paul urge us to work as if unto the Lord if the work we were doing was completely insignificant? In studying this idea of God's design for vocation, I discovered seven kinds of work that God invites us to do as a reflection of the work He does. I'll list a few examples, but I think you could fit most occupations into one of these seven categories.

Creative work. God fashioned the world and revealed himself through it. If you're a musician or an author, if you're an architect or a photographer, if you're a graphic designer or an artist of any kind—you are participating in God's creative work. You're fashioning the world and revealing God's glory through it.

Provisional work. God created systems for sustaining the world he had created. If you work in utilities, trades, farming or engineering, you are doing God's providing work. Business and commerce is our world's system of generating and trading resources. If you're in business, you're doing God's work of providing for people.

Justice work. God is and always has been intent on bringing justice, correction and restoration to the world he created. If you work as a lawyer, judge or police officer, you are doing justice work.

Compassionate work. Jesus' ministry on earth showed us just how strongly God's heart beats with compassion. If you're a nurse, doctor, social worker, aid worker or counselor, you are doing God's compassionate work.

Revelatory work. God shows and reveals his truth to people. If you're a teacher or a scientist, if you're a journalist or a filmmaker, if you're a pastor or a missionary: your occupation is reflecting God's revelatory nature. You are participating in God's revelatory work.

Community Work. God designed people to live in community and relationship with one another, and he works to bring connection and unity. If you work in real estate and bring buyers and sellers together; if you work in the restaurant business where you serve people who gather over meals; if you're a civic leader or a city planner or community organizer—you are doing God's community work.

Service work. Throughout scripture, God is described as our helper, and Matthew 20:28 says that Jesus came not to be served, but to serve others. Whatever vocation you do that serves other people, from cleaning to customer service, you are doing God's service work.

You can probably think of people whose job fits one of the above categories but whose lives and work don't at all reflect God's purpose. Maybe you know a lawyer who acts very unjustly, or a teacher who taught you a lie instead of revealing truth—one that went deep into your soul and caused damage. Maybe you've talked with customer service representatives who seem bent on making your day as difficult as possible instead of serving you.

God created work, but sin ruined everything. Work stopped being worship, and it became drudgery, greed, power and toil. It became twisted and tainted and divorced from its created purpose. But because of the work that Jesus did on the cross, we are redeemed from sin and set free from the curse God placed on sin. When you choose to view your job as a piece of earth that God has given you to cultivate, you are doing redemptive work. You are restoring "occupation" to its original, sacred purpose, which is to reflect God's productive nature, and to participate in the creating and sustaining of the earth he gave us.

When we view Christ as our boss, our work has significance. And because we all share the same heavenly boss, we all have an equal opportunity to worship God with our work. Martin Luther King Jr. said, "If a man is called to be a street sweeper, he should sweep streets even as Michelangelo painted, or Beethoven composed music, or Shakespeare wrote poetry. He should sweep streets so well that all the hosts of heaven and earth will pause to say, 'Here lived a great street sweeper who did his job well.'"

Application Two: If work is worship, then your calling can be found in your work.

Verse six in Paul's instructions for work says that we should do the will of God from our hearts. The motivation for our work should come from a deep place within us. It should look less like an activity that we do for money and more like a calling that we fulfill for a purpose.

The idea that our calling can be found in our work is another mental shift for us, because we tend to separate the sacred and the secular into two categories. The sacred involves praying, going to church, and reading the Bible; the secular involves work and watching sports on television.

The church reinforces this separation by emphasizing the importance of jobs like church planting and missions over jobs that don't have an overtly spiritual purpose to them. For example, my friend John works as an IT specialist for a large company but senses God's leading towards overseas missions. The way we would generally describe this shift in John's occupation would suggest that John is just now receiving a *calling* from God. Information Technology at a corporation was a job; being a missionary is his calling. Sometimes changing the way we talk about things is the first step to really changing our perspective. So let's try this on for size: Every single person who has chosen to follow Jesus is a full-time minister, and every workplace is a mission field.

For example, imagine a school in your neighborhood that's filled with young children five days a week. How is God going to reach this diverse mission field? He takes a full-time minister—one with intelligence, leadership ability, and perhaps a little more patience than the average person—and he carefully places her into the public school system to live out a *calling* as a public school teacher. Across town is yet another mission field full of strong, tough construction workers who, whether they know it or not, are reflecting God's heart for community by building homes. God takes a full-time minister, gives him a lot of muscles and maybe even a few tattoos, and then places him on site to live out a *calling* as a construction worker. I have two full-time minister friends who have a great talent for storytelling and technical skills such as editing and post-production. I don't know the first thing about film editing. It's no wonder that God dropped them (and not me) right in the middle of the film industry, where they live out their *calling* as filmmakers.

We know from scripture that children are close to God's heart. How is he going to reach them and show them his love? He takes a full-time minister and gives her some invisible superpowers, like the ability to do five things at one time, a sixth-sense for danger, and supernatural mouth spit that fixes everything. Then he drops her right into a family where she lives out her *calling* as a mother.

How we view our work is the only difference between engaging it as a toil or a calling. Are we going to offer our work as worship and do the will of God from our hearts? Or are we going to merely get through the day out of a sense of duty and need for a paycheck?

Application Three: If work is worship, then the Holy Spirit needs to be your CSO.

A CEO, of course, is a Chief Executive Officer. A CFO is a Chief Financial Officer. A CSO is what I call a Chief Strategy Officer. If you're going to go into work with the intent to worship, then you must be, as Paul says in verse seven, "wholehearted." You must be fully committed to what God wants you to do.

Jesus says in John 4:24, "God is spirit, and those who worship him must worship in spirit and in truth." God knows that we cannot worship him out of our own human energy. We need something supernatural and God-breathed in order to worship him. So before we start our workday and at various moments throughout it, our prayer should always be, "Holy Spirit, fill me." At some point during the week, you will face a co-worker's mean attitude. Unless you are filled with the Holy Spirit, you won't be able to navigate that situation with an attitude of worship. *Holy Spirit, fill me.*

You may work in an environment that requires a lot of compassion for people. If you think that you can depend on your own kindness day after day, you'll begin to feel your compassion dry up. To serve God wholeheartedly, you're going to need the Spirit of God working in you. *Holy Spirit, fill me.*

Maybe you work among people who aren't always ethical in their work. Cutting corners, laziness, dishonesty and backstabbing are often part of the employee culture. Your conscience and natural willpower will eventually falter, and when it does, pray: *Holy Spirit, fill me.*

One of the times I mostly clearly experienced the Holy Spirit working as my CSO was a few years ago when I was out of town speaking at a church. I had finished several services and had one service left when I felt a very clear impression on my heart that I needed to call home. I tried to reason the voice away, thinking, *I've done these services before and never called home between them. There's no reason to call.* But the impression didn't relent. *Call home.*

Eventually I relented and called my wife. She didn't answer, which was unusual, but of course there were plenty of reasons why she might not have been able to answer, and I needed to get ready for the next service. *Call home.* The impression wouldn't leave me. So I called my daughter, Rachel, and she answered by saying, "Dad, something's happened. Call mom." So I called Marie again, and this time she answered. She said she had just picked up our son at church camp and discovered his appendix had burst. He was bleeding internally and was being rushed into emergency surgery.

I hung up the phone and knew I had to get home. I explained to the pastor what was happening, so they put me in a car and rushed me to the airport. I had no idea how I was going to get a last minute flight, but I knew I needed to try.

If you've ever been to Los Angeles International Airport, you know what a madhouse it is. I walked into the terminal and saw every security line was backed up and every ticket counter was full. My anxiety rose as I thought about my child who was about to go into a life-saving operation while I was standing in long lines trying to catch a flight. As I stood there looking at all the over-crowded lines, an airline representative walked over to me and asked, "Can I help you?" I was shocked to be noticed and served so quickly by an airline representative, even though I wasn't standing in any line. I quickly explained my story. She said, "Come with me." She walked me over to a computer terminal, quickly typed into her computer and handed me a boarding pass. She then escorted me over to the front of security, ignoring the dirty looks we were both getting from other people in line. She walked me all the way to the gate to make sure that I would not miss my flight. As I boarded the plane, I turned around and, with complete amazement at what had just happened, said, "Thank you." I'll never forget what she said to me. She looked at me and said, "I'll pray for your son."

In that moment I saw everything that had just happened from a heavenly perspective. The Holy Spirit had urged me to call home; if I hadn't been listening, I wouldn't have known until much later that my son was going into surgery. The Holy Spirit then selected one of his full-time ministers in the airlines and positioned her to help me. Because she was listening and obedient, God's purpose for me was accomplished, and He was blessed by her wholehearted worship. To worship God wholeheartedly with our work, we need the Holy Spirit working in us.

Application Four: If work is worship, then I see God as the source of my reward.

It may seem like we work for our own reward, but our paychecks are often connected to the work of other people and not just our own effort. If our team does well, we see bonuses and raises. If our business flourishes, so do we. If our industry is doing well, that increases the chances that our business does well, which increases the chances that our team does well. And then of course there's that economy as a whole, which so often dictates our income. So your paycheck is dependent on your own performance, but also that of your team, your business, your industry, and the economy. If our livelihoods are that dependent on other people, consider how much more dependent were the "rewards" of a slave. Yet in verse eight, Paul offers this promise: God will reward you, *individually*, for the work that you do. If your work is an act of worship, God will reward you for the work you do. His reward is not tied to your team or industry, and it can't be taken away even in a troubled economy.

There are three ways God rewards us. First, God rewards us *materially*. When we get our paychecks, our very first response should be to thank God, because every single thing that we needed in order to earn our paycheck comes from him. The raw materials that went into whatever product your company sells comes from God. Any information, concept, mathematics, language or scientific process that your work depends on comes from God. If your job requires any physical labor (and yes, walking to the printer counts!), then your work is dependent on God, the Creator and Sustainer of your body. *Everything* material comes from God, so he is the true source of your material reward.

Second, God rewards us *internally*. When we live out our calling, our character changes and develops. I imagine that after the airline representative finished putting me on that plane, her entire day was elevated and her character was developed in some way as a result of living out her calling. Money can't equal the internal reward that Christ has for us when we offer our work as worship. And it's the internal stuff—character development, wisdom, experience—that God can use in your life to form Christ in you, the greatest reward.

Finally, God rewards us *eternally*. This reward is a bit more mysterious. Believing that God rewards us eternally requires a measure of faith that says, "Even though I don't fully understand how, the work God has given me to do isn't a waste. My life has value and meaning beyond me and beyond my time on earth. I don't know how he's going to use this or for what purpose, but I trust him." God's eternal rewards far outshines His material reward, even if we can't quite measure this side of heaven. Believing this is like being handed a blank contract and choosing to sign it and count on it. The only reason it would ever be smart to sign a blank contract would be if you know who wrote the contract and trust his intentions for you. Do you trust him?

Application Five: If work is worship, then people are the priority.

The final verse in the passage says that there is no favoritism in God's Kingdom. Every person has equal value to God. The workplace of this world, on the other hand, runs almost entirely on a system of favoritism. *It's not what you know; it's who you know.* In a job, more than any other situation, we work and position ourselves to be favored. Our livelihood depends on it! We work to make ourselves more valuable than the people we're competing against in order to secure our promotion. We look to build connections with people whom we can leverage. In short, we are operating in a system that views people as a commodity.

God looks on this twisted version of the good thing he created, and he says, "I show no favoritism." In other words, "My system is completely different than the system you're operating in." When work resumes its proper role in our lives as an act of worship, we remember that people have intrinsic value that isn't tied to what they can offer us, and that our worth isn't tied to a title or salary.

I have a friend who started a business on the south side of Chicago. When I think of people who see their jobs as a unique opportunity to worship God,

I think of this friend. Christ is his boss. He lives out his calling in the workplace. He is filled with the Holy Spirit. He very clearly sees God as the source of the success he's had in business. But I think the most powerful way that he worships God with his work is how he makes people the priority.

The area where my friend started his tea importing business is in one of the worst neighborhoods in Chicago. The unemployment rate among young men is over fifty percent, and a high percentage of them end up in prison. When he hires one of these men, he says, "This is my offer. I'm only going to give you a job here for three or four years. During that time, we will help you obtain your next level of education, whether that is a high school diploma, a college degree, or a certificate from a trade school. You tell us what you want to do with your life, and by the time you finish working here, I want to see you in the career of your choice." My friend sees his business as a means to help underprivileged young people reach their dreams.

Maybe you don't own your own business, and maybe you don't immediately see how you could be making this kind of a difference in your work. But begin praying about it. How does God want to build his kingdom here on earth, in your workplace, through you?

Thank God it's Monday

My wife and I have a good friend who's a nurse. Being a nurse in America is no easy job. She work long shifts and difficult hours in emotionally intense situations, and the demands placed on her are often much greater than the resources and support she's given.

But our friend is fully committed to the idea that her work is an act of worship to God. Before every shift she prays, "Lord, fill me with your Spirit. Remind me that this is my time of worship, that you're my boss, and that there are people here who really matter to you. Help me to do my job with Christ-like character."

With a prayer and attitude like that, whom do you think is sought out for counsel and comfort when another nurse is going through a divorce, or when someone's daughter goes off the deep end, or when a loved one falls ill? Our friend, of course. She shines and reflects Jesus all day at work, and people are drawn to her. As a result, she has meaningful conversations with people, which often lead to an invitation to church or a decision to follow Jesus. But it all begins with her decision to view her work as an act of worship, and by loving and prioritizing people so much that they have to ask her why her work-life is so different from others.

The next time you go into work, *how* are you going to go into work? With what attitude or perspective? Will you see work as yet another day of toil and drudgery? Will you go in determined to advance yourself at whatever cost? Will you count the minutes until you can leave?

If you're done with that old way of working and you're ready to begin seeing work different, then try this: When you pull into the driveway at work, take a moment to acknowledge Christ, your true boss, the way you will check in with your earthly boss. "What's on the agenda today? What do you have for me?" When you walk in the door, don't walk in like you're on shift; walk in like you're on a mission. Walk in believing that you're answering a divine calling. Throughout your day, but especially in moments when you feel weak or drained, breathe in a quick prayer. *Holy Spirit, fill me.* He will. When you receive your paycheck, or when you experience a moment of internal reward, immediately give thanks to God as your source.

And with every person you come in contact with—whether that be your boss who's handling promotions or the person who sweeps the floors—ask God for his eyes to see the intrinsic value of that person in his kingdom. Ask to be a reflection of his love, so that your interaction might take them one step closer toward discovering and knowing Jesus.

Life Application

1. How can you begin to see Jesus as your workplace boss?

2. What kind of prayer would enable you to be lead by the Holy Spirit while you are at your job?

3. Have you thought about the rewards God gives you through your work? Which ones have you seen?

4. How can your work be viewed as a divine calling from God?

5. How might God be establishing his Kingdom on earth through your occupation?

6. Who do you work with that doesn't know Jesus, and how can you reach them?

Chapter Two

Success

But the path of the righteous is like the morning sun, shining ever brighter till the

full light of day.

Proverbs 4:18

How do you define "success" in your walk with Christ?

Success is an emotionally loaded word, isn't it? If you feel a little anxious when you hear it, you're not alone. Most of us think that "to succeed" means to finally get to a place where all that we dreamed of and hoped for has come to pass. It's a place where we feel like we have finally crossed the finish line and can take a rest. We want to feel that secure feeling that we've *arrived* in life. With that sense of arrival, we expect to feel peace, satisfaction, enjoyment, freedom and security.

When it comes to our faith, "success" is another word for "perfection". We think everyone, including God, expects us to be perfect. We believe we will be successful Christians once we reach a high level of devotion and maturity. We view our spiritual journey as a linear grid from imperfect to perfect. Unfortunately, our unconscious grid looks something like this...

1   2   3   4   5   6   7   8   9   10

IMPERFECT – IMPERFECT – IMPERFECT –PERFECT

...Which means we spend a lot of time feeling like failures. The pressure to be instantly and consistently flawless in our spirituality can be so strong that it's tempting to resort to faking it.

When you get saved, let's say you're at a "3". But everyone else in your life looks like a Christian at a "9". Immediately you're tempted to pretend being a "9", rather than grow genuinely to be a "4". And when you fake being a "9", not having grown through the stages, you will eventually fall hard. When you're only looking forward to being a "9", you never look behind you at those just beginning to grow, needing your help, as you have just gone through the growth steps they are now facing. When, at some point, you think you've become a "9" then the temptation is to quit growing. You've arrived. You've crossed the finish line of being a successful Christian. You've forgotten that when you get to the number "10", God lets you peek around the corner and see that the numbers "11 through 5 bazillion" still exist to grow into. There is never an end to growing in Christ. There is only a next step. Success is not about crossing some imaginary finish line, but about growing into the next step of your walk with Christ.

I have a friend who made the decision to follow Jesus in his late twenties. A few weeks after his conversion, he told me that he was reading his Bible for an hour every morning, praying for an hour every evening, and was participating in several ministries. I was amazed at his high level of commitment, but later I found out that he wasn't telling me the truth. I don't think he intended to lie, but I think he had a picture of what a "Good Christian" does, and he felt the need to at least appear like he was doing things right.

It's not uncommon for even mature Christians to do this, too, though perhaps more subtly than my friend. Have your ever implied something about your devotional or prayer life that made you appear more "advanced" spiritually? Or have you ever put a godly spin on something that you thought sounded too earthy or mundane for Christian conversation? Or have you ever told someone that you had been praying for them when you actually hadn't—thinking that you could make up for the deception by praying later, and that by saying it now it would make you look like a successful Christian? I don't think we simply want to look good in front of other people. I think we really want to feel what it will be like when we finally "arrive" as a successful Christian, and so we pretend we're already there. The ridiculous part—and we all know it's ridiculous—is that we do this not only for our own sake, but also for God's sake. We want him to see our show.

We disbelieve or forget that we were completely redeemed, saved and accepted in the very the moment we turned to Jesus. We believe that the gospel is only the first step, when really the gospel is the entire story. What follows our moment of salvation is the process of spiritual formation—of becoming more and more like Jesus. Proverbs 4:18 describes the path of the righteous as the light of the sun, growing brighter and brighter until the full day. We're on a journey of following Jesus. We are not expected to perform and be perfect for Him.

So what does this journey of pursuing God look like, and how can we move forward authentically? In the first verses of Luke 18, Jesus tells the story of a widow who continues to petition a judge with her request. Luke gives away the meaning of the parable by saying, "Jesus told his disciples a parable to show them that they should always pray and not give up." After sharing this short parable about persistently seeking after God, Jesus wanted to make sure that no one got the wrong idea. Luke writes in verse nine, "To some who were confident in their own righteousness and looked down on everyone else, Jesus told his parable."

Luke 18:10-13: "Two men went to the temple to pray, one a Pharisee and the other a tax collector. The Pharisee stood by himself and prayed: God, I thank you that I am not like other people—robbers, evil doers, adulterers—or even like this tax collector. I fast twice a week and give ten percent of all I get." But the tax collector stood at a distance. He would not even look up to heaven but beat his breast and said, 'God, have mercy on me, a sinner.' I tell you that this man, rather than the other, went home justified before God.'"

This story takes place at Israel's most holy site, the temple. Jesus describes two people at the opposite end of the religious spectrum. The Pharisee is a respected religious leader, while the tax collector is a despised member of society. Tax collectors worked for the Roman government and were notoriously corrupt, so Jewish people hated Jewish tax collectors.

This story would have surprised Jesus' listeners for a couple reasons. First, the Jews listening to Jesus tell the story would not have been used to hearing a Pharisee praying out loud the way Jesus described in this story. Pharisees would have often thought such things, but they wouldn't pray in a way that revealed such external arrogance. And tax collectors simply wouldn't pray at the temple. Jesus was getting everyone's attention with this story by expressing, "I see beyond the external and into the heart."

The problem with the Pharisee is that he really believes what he's saying. He thinks that by performing in front of God, he qualifies before God. He fasts twice a week. He tithes on all of his income. Notice that both of those actions are external matters of *doing* and not internal matters of *being*. He doesn't say that he's full of peace and love and patience, and he doesn't marvel at the things God has done in his life. One of the clues that you might be pursuing God self-righteously is if you're constantly measuring the things you can do out of your own strength and discipline rather than worshipping God for his work in you. Another clue is that you are always comparing your spirituality to those who seem less spiritual than you are.

Then the Pharisee gives thanks to God, but he does it in a very strange way. He doesn't thank God *for* anything (for his love, his mercy, his blessings, or so on). Instead he words his prayer so he can talk about himself again. "Thank you God THAT..." Thank you God that I'm not a robber! Thank you God that I'm not an adulterer! He compares himself to the worst of people in order to elevate himself even further. When you compare yourself to others, you will always find someone worse than you. No matter where you are on the spectrum of sinful to righteous living, there is always someone who is doing better and there's always someone who's doing it worse.

The Pharisee is a picture of someone who is performing for God, and who believes he is responsible for his spiritual status and achievement. The opposite could also be true. Rather than bragging how great we are, we could always state how miserable we are. "I'm not good enough. I haven't arrived yet. I'm a failure." These statements of shame, just like the statements of status, also are a rejection of the gospel. Anytime we credit ourselves with the ability to perform our way to justification, whether we think we're succeeding or failing, we're rejecting the gospel.

The tax collector in Jesus' story is the opposite of the Pharisee in every way. He is standing at a distance from the temple, which shows humility. He acknowledges that he's in utter need of God's mercy, he cries out for forgiveness, and then he goes home.

One Sunday a young man came to find me after a service. He had prayed to receive Christ a month before, and I was happy for the chance to follow up with him, but I could tell right away something was wrong. (He was crying, for one thing, which was my first clue.)

He said, "I've got a horrible confession to make. You know I got saved a month ago? Well, I have a girlfriend, and since getting saved I haven't stopped sleeping with her." I paused for a second before responding. Then I said, "That's great!" He look at me confused and said, "I thought that was a bad thing."

I responded, "That you're sleeping with your girlfriend? Absolutely. That doesn't honor God, it doesn't honor your relationship, and you need to deal with it. But the fact that you had the courage to come tell me about it instead of hiding... the fact that you'd be vulnerable enough to expose this part of your life and seek the Lord in it... that's truly great. That's a huge step forward in following Jesus, and I want to celebrate it."

Confession is one of the ways that we authentically move forward in our relationship with the Lord. This young man felt genuinely sorry about the sin in his life and he was willing to expose it even though it wouldn't make him look very spiritual. Confession brings the shameful areas of our life out into the light, where God can heal and redeem. Confession also protects us from becoming full of judgment towards others, like the Pharisee. When you're in the practice of presenting your sins and admitting your need for grace, you don't really feel the desire to condemn other people for their sins and their need for grace.

Jesus said that it was the tax collector, not the Pharisee, who was justified. "Justified" means that we have been made perfect in the eyes of God. It means that our sins are forgiven and wiped clean. A lot of us have a picture of Judge God who finds our file, reads it, and then strikes his gavel with a benevolent, "Your sins are forgiven, because of what Jesus has done for you." But Hebrews 10:17 (quoting Jeremiah 31) says that God "remembers our sins no more." So maybe a better picture of justification is God in his robes, searching through case files, saying, "You know what? I don't see a charge against you in here. Why are you here? You're free to go."

Jesus says that the tax collector beats his chest, calls out for mercy, and then goes home, justified. You don't have to stay at the temple, begging. You don't have to live in a place of despair. The moment you come to the cross is the moment your sins are forgiven and remembered no more. There is no moment that you become perfect and worthy of God's salvation; there is only the moment when God's grace and strength is made perfect in you. Then it's time to go home. In other words, it's time to move on and move forward in your life.

Paul writes in 2 Corinthians 3:18, "And we all, who with unveiled faces contemplate the Lord's glory, are being transformed into his image with ever-increasing glory, which comes from the Lord, who is the Spirit." Wherever you are in your journey of faith, you are reflecting God's glory. Part of Jesus is shining out of you, and in your transformation (your process of being changed and changed, over and over), that light is growing brighter and brighter. You don't have to perform, and there is no finish line. The "ten" on your unconscious grid of perfection won't feel like an arrival at all, because remember the numbers eleven through eternity come after it. Spiritual transformation is an ongoing process, not a challenge to be mastered. And we can move forward from wherever we are with a sense of peace and security.

When I was dating Marie, I'd often meet her for lunch downtown Chicago where she worked. I loved those lunches, but there was always an edge to them, especially in the beginning. I was always trying to monitor how she felt about me, and I was always trying to figure out what the next step in our relationship should be. Was she ready to commit to me? Did she feel the same way about me as I felt about her? We continued to grow in our relationship, and eventually she did agree to marry me. A couple weeks after we got married, Marie mentioned, "I really enjoy having lunch with you, Joel. I hope you'll still come downtown to meet me on my breaks." I'll never forget that very first lunch with Marie after she became my wife. The edge I had felt on our previous dates was completely gone. Whatever had been unclear or tentative had been made clear and final. It was finished and done. We could move forward in pursuing each other and our relationship, but we could do it in a place of total security and acceptance. We had entered into a covenant relationship.

Assurance, peace, security—these are all good things that we want when we don't have them. But once we do have them, there's a tendency to begin taking what we have for granted. The thing we wanted and desired so much can become commonplace to us. Maybe you've seen this happen with your kids around Christmastime. Before Christmas there's a toy they want more than anything else in the world, and you'd think that all of their wildest dreams had come true when they open it. They spend the day playing with it, admiring it, and thanking you for it. But where is that toy a month later?

Is it still on a shelf of honor in their room? Are they still playing with it every spare second? Are they still gushing with gratitude? Or is it lying around with the rest of their possessions, another commonplace "thing" that they own?

Life with Jesus should never become commonplace. We can follow him with assurance, peace and security, but following him should also feel like discovery. When you wake up in the morning, ask, "What do you have for me today, Jesus? What are you up to that I can be a part of?"

Redefining Success

A successful journey with Christ—a whole, authentic, alive journey with Christ—starts at the cross. 1 Peter 2:24 says that Jesus carried our sins so that we could live the right way. The cross made us spiritually, emotionally and physically whole. A successful journey with Jesus begins by responding with love to his gift of grace.

But here's the twist. An authentic journey with Jesus also *continues* by responding with love to his gift of grace. We don't start with love, gratitude and celebration and then move into performance. A lot of us are like the performing Pharisee than we want to think. We read that story and think, "Thank God that I'm not like that arrogant Pharisee!" We think in the same way the Pharisee thought about the tax collector.

We start with the cross, and we continue with the cross. We never graduate from gospel. We pick up our cross and follow Jesus, not just as a means of sacrifice, but also as a means of gratitude for what the cross has done for us. We have a God who loves us and who asks us to follow him in a simple way. Not an easy way, but a simple way. He's created a path for us if we'll only take it. Paul says that his whole life was wrapped up in that promise of transformation. He wasn't reaching for a final number or a moment of success; he was reaching for Jesus. Philippians 3:13: "Brothers and sisters, I do not consider myself yet to have taken hold of it. But this is one thing I do: Forgetting what is behind and straining toward what is ahead, I press on toward the goal…"

How do we press on toward any goal? How do we run any race? We take the next step. That's the only thing you can do in a race—take the next step. There's no shortcut or leap or magic formula; there is only step after step after step.

Jesus was absolutely brilliant at nudging people toward their next step. He didn't say, "Peter, leave your fishing nets. I want you to be the rock upon which I'll build my church." Instead he said, "Peter, put down your net and follow me, and I'll teach you a new way to fish." Jesus only gave Peter a look at his next step. When Jesus met Zacchaeus, he didn't call into the tree, "Repent and be saved!" Instead he said, "Let's eat a meal together." Again, he gave Zacchaeus the next step for his life. When Jesus was visiting with Martha and Mary, he saw where Martha was at in her spiritual journey, and he invited her to put some things down and rest in him for a bit. Paul had a pretty dramatic, divine first encounter with Jesus. But Jesus didn't say, "Paul, give up everything to suffer and die for me." He said, "Go to the dessert and start learning what it means to follow me." Jesus gave Paul his next step.

What is Jesus nudging you toward? What's the next step in that journey? If you think he's nudging you toward becoming a witness at your work, your next step probably isn't to go from person to person preaching a sermon on the gospel. The next step might be to invite one co-worker out to lunch and build a friendship. If Jesus is nudging you to put down roots in a church, your next step likely isn't to immediately join five ministries. It's probably to start attending every week and join a small group. If Jesus is nudging you to begin taking the Bible more seriously, your next step probably isn't to apply at a seminary. But it might be to start reading scripture every morning, or to join a Bible study.

When I was growing up, prayer wasn't an easy discipline for me. But I knew it was important and I felt God nudging me to grow in my prayer life. So I put structures in place, one at a time, and eventually I developed a practice of prayer that has been a foundation in my devotional life. But there's always another step, right? One day I was reading Psalm 119 and came across the line, "Oh how I love your law! I meditate on it all day long." Meditate on God's word all day long? I could go hours without even thinking about the fact that God is present with me. My next step was to set an alarm on my phone for every five hours, and every time it went off, I took a moment to acknowledge Jesus and his presence in my life.

Be intentional about your next step. Truly seek the Lord on it, and then stick with it. Don't be limited by the things we naturally put in the "spiritual" category, like prayer, or Bible study, or church involvement. Think about the totality of your life, because Jesus wants to be involved in every area. Maybe your next step with Jesus has something to do with a relationship, or your parenting, or your career, or your bank account, or your neighborhood. I once took kite surfing lessons as my next step with

See. Life. Different.

Jesus. Walking with Jesus often calls for discipline and picking things up, but it also calls for celebration and letting things go.

Another clue that you might be pursuing God out of self-righteousness is if you find yourself comparing and judging more often than learning and celebrating. Letting go of comparison and judgment is truly one of best ways of moving out of "performance" and into "growth."

If you're ready to leave the performance and perfectionism behind and start moving forward in an authentic and growing walk with Christ, here are three steps you can take.

First: think of one way that you have grown in faith over the past year. Whether it's a discipline that you grew in, such as prayer, or a fruit of the Spirit that you believe matured inside of you, such as patience or kindness—write down one way that you experienced forward movement. Celebrate it. Give thanks for it. Acknowledge the work of Jesus in you.

Second: pray and ask God to reveal an area of your life and faith he wants you to move forward in next, and then seek him for the next step. Write that down too.

Finally, look at whatever you wrote down, and don't immediately do it. You *can* do it, of course. No one is stopping you. If it looks helpful and exciting, and if it's something that you'd like to embark on in your journey with Jesus, then by all means! That's the end goal of what spiritual formation should feel like: a joyful opportunity to grow closer to Jesus and become more like him. But if you're someone with a powerful urge to perform, then the most important next step you can take is to attack your belief that you need to perform for God. Wait until you know that next step has nothing to do with God's acceptance of you. Once you're heart is in the right place, then take that next step with joy, faith and delight.

A few years ago I was waiting to board a plane and had a short conversation with the man next to me. I found out he was a believer, so we chatted a bit about faith and ministry. Then we boarded the plane and sat down in our seats several rows apart. I fly quite a bit, but unfortunately I don't enjoy it at all. It's something I have to do, so I do it. To get through my flights as painlessly as possible, I typically enter into "cave" mode. I bring a book, newspaper or headset, go into my own little world, and then come out of it when I'm back on the ground.

About ten minutes into this particular flight, I turned around and saw the guy I had been previously talking to, now fully engaged in conversation with the person next to him. They were talking and laughing and clearly having a very dynamic conversation. I turned to the guy sitting next to me to examine the possibility of starting up a conversation, but there was no vibe there whatsoever. I flipped open my newspaper again and went back in my cave.

Ten minutes later I looked back and saw this guy with his Bible out, pointing at specific verses. Right there on the airplane! I turned back at the guy sitting next to me: he barely glanced at me, so I took that as a hint that he didn't want to talk. A few minutes later I looked back and the man was now praying with the person seated next to him. I didn't even look at the guy next to me. I certainly felt inspired and convicted by the experience, and I knew there were two ways I could reflect on it. If my walk with Christ is a performance, then clearly I had just failed in comparison to my brother several rows back. But if my walk with Christ is a growth process, if I've been justified and saved and am being transformed, then that plane ride was not only a life-changing experience for the man who had accepted Christ; it was also a learning experience for me. In was another mark on my path of discovering and following Jesus. I learned that I wanted to grow in boldness and obedience even when I'm feeling uncomfortable.   How would you have gotten off that plane, if you were me? Would you have left feeling like a failure of a Christian? Or would you have left celebrating the lesson God taught?

Life Application

1. How do you try to prove yourself as a successful Christian?

2. How do you at times "pretend" to be a better Christ-follower than you are?

3. Why do you feel compelled to be successful for God?

4. What would it feel like if you let go of the guilt and burden you carry for failing to be a perfect Christian?

5. What is the next step of growth God is asking you to take?

Chapter Three

People

Still other seed fell on good soil. It came up and yielded a crop, a hundred times

more than was sown.

Luke 8:8

Winters in California are much nicer than winters in Illinois, but there are a few things I miss about blustery, gray Chicago in January. For example, I miss one of my favorite winter spectator sports, which is watching people from warm regions try to drive through snow. It's a point of pride for Chicagoans that we can drive in just about any weather. Whenever I saw someone in snow, rocking their car back and forth, trying to spin their way out of a snowdrift and only digging themselves further in, my first thought was always, "Probably not from around here."

Of course even the most Midwestern of us can get stuck in the snow. Watching drivers spin their tires is, to me, an accurate picture of how we can sometimes feel in our lives and in our walk with Christ. We get stuck. No matter what we do, we can't seem to get unstuck. The harder we try, the more frustrated we get.

Not only can we find ourselves stuck, but often we get stuck in how we view the people in our lives. We sort people into two preliminary categories: people we like and get along with, and people we don't like and don't get along with. For those in that second category, we see two options: accept who they are, or try to change them. If we fail at doing either of those things, then we tend to give up on people or even abandon them. But Jesus saw people different.

Jesus' sermon about the famer sowing seeds contains profound truth about the kingdom of God and the nature of human hearts. Most of the time we read it and immediately think of evangelism, but it also has a lot to say about why we find ourselves "stuck" in various areas of our lives, and how we can live our lives with Christ "unstuck."

While a large crowd was gathering and people were coming to Jesus from town after town, he told this parable: "A farmer went out to sow his seed. As he was scattering the seed, some fell along the path; it was trampled on, and the birds ate it up. Some fell on rocky ground, and when it came up, the plants withered because they had no moisture. Other seed fell among thorns, which grew up with it and choked the plants. Still other seed fell on good soil. It came up and yielded a crop, a hundred times more than was sown." When he said this he called out, "Whoever has ears to hear, let him hear." (Luke 8:4-8)

Notice that Jesus was speaking to a diverse group of people. "A large crowd" comprised of people from various towns means he wasn't speaking to a specific group, such as the Pharisees or the disciples. This was a message for everyone. Also notice, because of the time and place, he was speaking to people who understood agriculture. He was speaking to a farming community. However, farming then was very different than how we picture farming today. When we picture farms, we see vast fields and big tractors. But in sustenance farming, each person had his own small plot of land, which is how people grew their food. If they had anything left over, they traded it for something in the marketplace.

So the people in Jesus' audience weren't familiar with different kinds of soil in a hypothetical way. They had real experience with people trampling over a certain path across their plot, with that ground becoming hard, and with their harvest being affected. Palestinian ground was rocky; they had seen how the plant came up like it might live but died off as soon as any weather came. They had patches of land that were particularly weedy and thorny. They knew which corner of their plot had the best soil and the best harvest. This is the image of soil and farming that Jesus' audience would have had when they heard this sermon.

After Jesus was finished speaking, his disciples did what they often did. They asked for an explanation. Jesus responded by reminding them of the purpose behind his parables, which is to explain the secrets of the kingdom. The story of the farmer tells us something about how the kingdom works in people's hearts. It's not a simplistic message about heaven and hell, and it's not a statistical analysis that one in four people will get saved. It's about having the kingdom fully inside of you, flourishing and growing. It's a lesson about the people in our lives, and how we can help them.

After the disciples asked Jesus for the interpretation, Jesus did something he almost never did. He gave it to them! His disciples must have been thrilled. Jesus explained that the seed in the parable is the word of God. The word, of course, is the same "word" from John 1:1, "In the beginning there was the word." The word, or the seed, is Jesus. He is planted in our hearts.

Those of us who know Jesus might wonder who wouldn't want him. Who wouldn't want eternal life? Who wouldn't want the peace that passes all understanding and every other good thing that life with Jesus offers? The seed, Jesus, is perfect. There's nothing wrong with the seed. But no matter how perfect a seed, if the soil isn't right nothing will grow.

In verse twelve, Jesus starts to unpack what each type of soil symbolizes, beginning with the soil that has been beaten down into a path. "Those along the path are the ones who hear, and the devil comes and takes away the word from their hearts, so that they may not believe and be saved."

When I was in college I worked as a gas station attendant in a dangerous neighborhood. My coworker and I sat in a bulletproof glass box, and we exchanged money with customers by sliding a drawer in and out. This coworker of mine would typically show up to our shift stoned out of his mind, which often led to very interesting conversations. (The more stoned, the more interesting.) But one day he came in entirely sober, and I decided that this was probably my window of opportunity to talk about Jesus with him. I started by asking for his story.

He began, "I had a great family until I turned thirteen." I asked what happened when he turned thirteen. He said, "My parents started going to church, and my life became hell." Surprised and intrigued, I asked him to explain. He said that before he turned thirteen, he had a loving mom and dad, but that as soon as they started going to church, nothing he ever did was good enough for them anymore. Everything was met with disdain and disapproval. He began to get walked on, and walked on, and walked on. He told me, "Joel, if you believe that God is love, you're an idiot." Suddenly I understood why every seed of love or truth I had thrown at this guy had bounced back at me.

What happens to people when they get continually walked on? Like soft ground that gets trampled, their hearts get hard and packed down as a way of protecting themselves from getting hurt again. Maybe this is your story. Maybe you've been walked on so many times that the soil of your heart is hard, and you feel stuck.

In verse thirteen, Jesus explains another kind of soil. "Those on the rocky ground are those who received the word with joy when they hear it, but they have no root. They believe for a while, but in the time of testing they fall away."

When I was just starting to work as a pastor, a friend of mine asked me if I would visit his friend in prison. I went and got to know this inmate, and I started visiting him every few weeks over the course of a year. One day there was a knock on my door, and I opened it to see this inmate on my front step. In all honesty, I was a little nervous about having him at my house, and I quickly prayed, *God, please don't let this be my Good Samaritan moment.* After greeting me he explained that he was on parole, and he asked if I would come to a party he was throwing. I agreed. *A party. I can always go to a party.*

The following week I showed up at a party. Picture one scrawny pastor and sixty ex-cons all crammed into an apartment. Half of the guys seemed like nice, decent men. (The other half did not.) But my friend was so impressed that I came to his party that he found me afterwards to ask if I would get coffee with him later that week. When we sat down to coffee, he started our conversation with a statement any pastor would hope for after seven months of jail visits and one uncomfortable party. He said, "You know this whole God thing? I think I'm interested." We ended up praying together, and the next week he showed up at church and began attending regularly.

Over time, though, I noticed him coming to church less and less. Then one day I got a letter from him saying, "Dear Joel, I'm really sorry to tell you this, but I'm going back to prison. Thanks for trying to help me." His letter explained that he had never been able to find a job as an ex-con, and his financial troubles mounted. Some demons from his past life showed up with an opportunity to make money illegally, and he made bad decisions.

His heart was burdened with troubles like soil burdened with rocks, and there wasn't room for the seed of Jesus to take root in his life.

Sometimes the troubles of life become so overwhelming that we can't seem to find a way out. Whether they're troubles of our own making or just the stuff of life, they pile up, one on top of the other. Maybe this is your story right now. You go to bed and wake up with your concerns. You know and believe in Jesus, but there just isn't room for his kingdom to take root inside you. For many parents, this is the status of your children. They are overwhelmed with life's problems as they try to figure so much out at such a young age, and they can't quite seem to fit Jesus into their focus. Many of the people in our lives have serious troubles, and they struggle to remain in faith because of those troubles.

Jesus describes another type of person in verse fourteen: "The seed that fell among thorns stands for those who hear, but as they go on their way they are choked by life's worries, riches and pleasures, and they do not mature." This may very well be the standard soil of our Western lives. Ours is a society that's consumed with riches and pleasures and the anxious striving that comes with both.

I recently went to the movies for the first time in a few years. After paying a ridiculous price for a ticket to sit in a seat and be entertained for two hours, I wanted a drink and snack. The options for popcorn and coke aren't small, medium and large anymore; they're large, extra large and enormous. And of course, only the truly enormous size comes with free refills, so I decided it was the better deal. Out came a vat of popcorn so large I could have bathed in it, as well as a drink so tall that it took more than a little maneuvering to carry both at the same time. The straw on the drink was extra long so that I didn't have to be bothered to lift the cup. I could just dip my head down a bit and slurp.

That simple experience of going to the movies teaches our unconscious something. *We are entitled to as much as we want.* It doesn't matter whether we get a refill or throw away half the food… *We deserve exactly as much as we want.*

Think about buying something like a new smart phone. Along with the excitement of getting the latest and greatest is the tinge of anxiety that comes with knowing that it will be outdated in no time at all. Buying a big TV is no better, because they'll add a few inches to the next model. We now see more advertisements in one year than people fifty years ago did in their lifetime, and each and every segment is teaching us to be discontent with what we have. We're entitled, and we're discontent—a toxic cocktail.

For many of us, this is our story. We're weighed down with bills we can't afford and desires we can't attain, and like thorns wrapped around a seed, the fullness of the kingdom gets choked out. We're stuck. Many of the people in our lives are in this position as well.

In verse fifteen Jesus shows us one last type of person when he says, "But the seed on good soil stands for those with a noble and good heart, who hear the word, retain it, and by persevering produce a crop." The plant doesn't just appear the moment it's dropped into good ground; no, it grows over time through a process of perseverance. The plant must endure weather and winds, and it still needs sunshine and water and care. But good soil is hearty enough for that process, and in time, there will be a crop.

Here is the unspoken point that I think we often miss in this story. This is Jesus' lesson about people that he wanted his disciples to learn: *Soil can change.* People's hearts can change. And for the people in our lives, we are called to be soil changers.

A farmer who haphazardly throws seeds on soil isn't a very experienced or wise farmer. First he works and prepares the land. In fact, he will spend far more time preparing the ground for seed than he will spend sowing. He's going to till the path until it's soft, he's going to rake out the rocks, and he's going to kill the weeds and vines and thorns. Sometimes land is stubborn. Sometimes the rocks return and the weeds keep coming back. But he continues this process, over and over, patiently and faithfully. This is how Jesus wants us to work with people.

If your focus is just on throwing seed, you probably aren't going to see the results you're praying for, whether you're praying for breakthrough in your own life or in the life of someone else. I know many sincere Christians married to unbelievers, and they pray and believe and throw seed constantly, wondering why they never see change. The seed is perfect but the soil isn't right.

I believe our calling as believers is to be soil changers. Our job is not to do the work of the seed. Our job is to make sure the soil of people's hearts is ready to receive the seed, Jesus.

Jesus lived with an incurable belief that people could change. He saw beyond the rocks, weeds and thorns to the rich soil beneath. In Zacchaeus, a crook and a thief, he saw a generous giver in the kingdom of God. In

51

Mary, a prostitute, he saw a great worshiper. In Paul, a persecutor of the church, he saw an apostle, a builder of the church. If the soil of their hearts could change, whose couldn't?

How did Jesus change soil? In one story Jesus and his disciples came across a man who had been completely outcast from his village. There was a spirit of evil over him, and he had been made to live in chains in a cemetery, where no one would have anything to do with him. The first thing the man wants to do when he meets Jesus is pick a fight, which is a telltale sign of hard soil. (When you encounter someone who leads antagonistically, remember to engage the person, not the fight. Hurting people hurt people, and you get to choose whether to respond to the person or react to the way they're lashing out.) Jesus reached out and embraced this man, delivering him from evil. *Hard soil is softened by unconditional grace and love.*

Back in the 80s we didn't know very much about HIV and AIDS, and there was a horrible stigma attached to the disease. One morning at the end of a service, a man walked toward me down the center aisle of the church. I could tell by his appearance that he was in a late stage of the disease. I asked God what he wanted me to do or say, but I sensed that I should not say a word. Instead, when he reached me at the front, I simply put my arms around him. He was stiff as a board for several long seconds, and then he suddenly melted in my arms and began to sob on my shoulder. I could physically feel the condition of his heart soften and change.

In another story, Lazarus falls ill and his family reaches out to Jesus for help, but Jesus gets there to late to heal him. One of the sisters meets Jesus at the front of the house. She's overwhelmed with her troubles, devoid of faith and joy, full of despair. What does Jesus do? He addresses her trouble. He raises Lazarus from the dead, turning a funeral into a celebration. Jesus changed their soil by helping solve their crisis.

When my daughter was seventeen years old, she heard about a remote village in Northern India that was in dire poverty. Churches that had attempted to reach out to this area had given up, because whenever missionaries tried to enter, the villagers would throw stones at them. The nearest school was a four-hour walk away, so the kids didn't go to school and the cycle of illiteracy and poverty continued. Then a twenty-three year old Indian woman entered the village, saying, "I just want to help. Let me teach your kids." Over the next three years she gained the trust of this village, and eventually she was single-handedly teaching over eighty children. My daughter heard this woman's story and felt God leading her to raise the money to build a school in this village.

After the school was built, my family was invited to the dedication ceremony. In a moment I will never forget, the elder of the community got up and looked at the young Indian woman who had been teaching their children. He said, "I am so ashamed. On behalf of this village, I ask your forgiveness. When you came, we had no idea the love that you were bringing to us." Then he asked me to pray. I stood in front of hundreds of people who used to throw stones at Christians, and I watched them bow their heads in honor as I prayed to the Lord Jesus Christ. By helping solve their problem, their hearts became soft to the love of Christ.

Soil can change. One young woman was willing to give her life to help an impoverished, illiterate community. Unlike the well-meaning missionaries who went before her, she didn't go in throwing seed. She went in with a shovel. She began digging up the problems that had been choking the kingdom from taking root. *Rocky soil is transformed with compassionate help.*

How do you change the soil of those who are so busy chasing wealth that they just don't have time for Christ? A "rich young ruler" once approached Jesus by saying something like, "Look here. I'm an A-plus religious man. I do everything right and I follow every rule. Am I in the kingdom?" Jesus replied (in more or less words), "That's all sounds great! There's just one more thing you need to do. You need to sell everything you have and give it to the poor." The young man walked away sad, stuck among the thorns. Like so many throughout the centuries, this rich young ruler could not accept Christ because of his soil condition.

I have a wealthy friend who was stuck in this way. He came to church about twice a month and seemed to sincerely love God, but there didn't ever seem to be any evidence of growth in his life. I found him one Sunday and said, "Hey, John! I heard about this great ministry that puts on long weekend events for children with learning disabilities, and I thought about you. I think you should underwrite one of the events. It's about five thousand dollars." He told me he wasn't interested, but I didn't give up. I made him feel really guilty about the whole thing until he finally agreed to sponsor the camp. Then I said, "This is great! But you can't just give money. You have to go be a part of the weekend."

Somehow I convinced him to take two days off work and spend a four-day weekend with kids who knew real and pure joy. For four days, he lived life beyond himself. After those four days, he looked at his bank account differently. He looked at his family different. He looked at his business different. What was the difference? The weeds that had been crowding out the seed of the kingdom had been removed. Jesus began to take real root in his life. That choice to participate in the weekend opened him up to a new way of living. Now he's involved in various projects and giving generously to causes around the world. He just needed an opportunity to experience a meaningful life by helping others. *Thorny soil is made rich by choosing an expansive, outward-focused life.*

Maybe you've been trampled on so many times that your heart is hard and impenetrable. Your step of faith is to trust God's love for you and to let him crack open your heart. The tilling process may be difficult, but there's soft soil beneath. Or maybe you have people in your life who need you to love them with an unconditional compassion, softening their hearts for Christ.

Maybe you're overwhelmed with troubles and the worries of life, either of your own making or not. Your step of faith is to tell someone and ask for help. Getting unstuck doesn't have anything to do with believing with more sincerity, because the problem isn't the seed. Your first step is to reach out with boldness for help, wherever you can find it, however God leads you. You may have to humbly allow someone else to wield the shovel for a while. Or maybe there is someone in your life asking for help. Your response may very well determine how they receive Christ.

Maybe your heart is so self-focused that you often feel anxiety and discontentment. God's kingdom can flourish in you too, but your soil has to change. Your step of faith is to choose self-sacrifice and generosity. Or maybe you know others consumed with riches. Find a way to help them have a meaningful moment helping others, and watch how their soil changes.

God puts people in our lives, both for our betterment and for theirs. Jesus never measured people by whether they were nice to him or not. He saw people for who they could be and helped them grow. This is now our work. We are soil changers.

Life Application

1. How would you describe the condition of your heart?

2. Who do you know that is hard-hearted, and what love and grace can you show them to soften their soil?

3. Who do you know that has so many troubles that they cannot focus on Christ, and what can you do to help them with their troubles?

4. Who do you know who is consumed with wealth, and how can you give them an opportunity to help other people?

5. How can you begin to see people as Jesus did – to see their potential and what they can become rather than what is wrong with them?

Joel Holm

Chapter Four

Stuff

"What should we do then?" asked the crowd. John answered them, "Anyone who has two shirts should share with one who has none, and anyone who has food should do the same."

Luke 3:10

For those of us trying to take the Bible seriously while living in a modern culture consumed with getting more wealth, "stuff" can be a difficult issue in life.

The church is very diverse in how it interprets the Bible's teachings on finances. From vows of poverty to gospels of prosperity to every moderate belief in between, it's hard to know what balance to strike, or whether balance is what we should be aiming for in the first place. We want to honor God with our money, but we're not sure where to begin or how to do it right.

A few years ago I was reading the life of Jesus in chronological order when I came across John the Baptist's teaching in Luke 3. John is essentially telling the crowd, "You've chosen a new way of life, so act like it. Be fruitful. Show the results." The crowd asks him how they should do that, and he responds, "Anyone who has two shirts should share with one who has none, and anyone who has food should do the same." I felt stirred when I read this passage. Giving is a part of my life. But the level of generosity that John was describing, and the kind of mindset I would need to have in order to follow it, is simply not how I think or live.

A couple things struck me about this "two shirt" picture that John used. First, John uses the word "share" instead of "give." The word "share" makes me think of when my kids were really young and I was constantly trying to teach them to share their things. Children somehow learn the word "mine" without any prompting whatsoever, and it's up to us as their parents to teach them how to open their chubby little death grips on stuff. Adults *give* and children *share*—if only because adults own things to give and children simply manage the items they've been given. Perhaps we should become more like children.

Sometimes we wonder why God blesses some and not others. But if everything that we have is a gift from God, then our stuff isn't our own. We're like children, managing the gifts that we've been given, choosing what to keep and what to share. This is a different way of thinking about our position as givers—not as one of ownership and power, but of gratitude and obedience.

Second, John describes an extreme but simple system: whatever you have, give half. It could be read even more extreme than that. He could be saying to give away *all* of our excess. "What do you need two shirts for? Give away the extra one!" (This from a man who lived in the wilderness wearing a garment made of camel's hair.)

But what interested me was this idea of a fifty-fifty way of living—of giving away half of everything that I have. What would it look like if I really lived that out?

The moment the thought entered my mind was the moment I knew God was challenging my family and I to do something very unusual. This is one of the hazards of reading God's word. He can plant a seed of an idea in your mind and keep it there until it grows into a full-blown, family-wide, month-long experiment that finds you paying for a stranger's haircut and researching how to get the best value on canned goods for a food bank. But I'm getting ahead of things.

The terms of the month-long exercise were simple. Whatever money we spent, we would give away the same amount in the same category. So if we bought a hundred dollars in food, we gave away a hundred dollars in food. Housing for housing. Medical costs for medical costs. It would have been much easier to tally up the month's spending and donate a lump sum to a charity or two, but I sensed there were some connections God wanted to make as I shared what I had with people who needed what I had. We also decided that we would maintain our normal lifestyle, and that we wouldn't monitor our income. Even though I believe that God blesses and rewards us when we give, I had a strong conviction that there were other things he wanted to teach me during the month of December.

Did I know that the idea was truly from God? No. But I hadn't been able to get it out of my mind, so why not try? Too often I decide not to try something because it's possible that the idea didn't really come from the Lord, but why not take the chance that it did? My wife and I decided to start it the very next day. We would spend the month of December matching every dollar we spent as a way to share with someone else. As I fell asleep that night, I felt nervous, excited, and a little bit ridiculous. But when I woke up, I had great energy for the exercise. I wanted to run out and buy something, just to get started.

That enthusiasm wouldn't last the entire month, but those first few days definitely gave me a rush. It was exciting to think of creative ways to give, and it was freeing to feel "license" to share. When I spent fifty dollars to repair my house, I gave fifty dollars to housing teens in Kenyan slums. When my wife got a haircut, she asked her stylist if she knew of someone who couldn't afford a haircut. Her stylist said that one of her long-term clients had just gone through bankruptcy and was depressed, so Marie paid for the haircut and left the stylist to set up the appointment with her client directly.

Early on I casually purchased eighty dollars worth of books at a church bookstore, completely forgetting about the experiment. When it hit me later, my first reaction was, "Shoot! Now I have to double that amount." But a split second later I thought about how I could give eighty dollars worth of books to a good friend of mine who leads a ministry in India. He probably never casually spends eighty dollars all at once anywhere, let alone at a bookstore, and I knew the resources would be valuable to his ministry. One second I was annoyed that I had to part with eighty dollars; the next second I was rejoicing over seeing that eighty dollars in someone else's hands.

On the fourth day I suffered a mild existential crisis while waiting in line at Starbucks, trying to figure out how I would match the six dollars I would spend on a cappuccino and a donut. Here's the thing: I love coffee. I'm not sure if that makes me a bad person or a superficial person or someone who's uncaring about farmers in the hills of Bolivia, but I really like coffee. The day before I hadn't felt any guilt whatsoever about buying eighty dollars worth of books at a Christian bookstore, but there I was feeling guilty about my six-dollar coffee purchase. It occurred to me that I was spending the equivalent of about two days' wages for many people in the world.

Talk about a gray and confusing subject. Does God care more about what I give to others or about what I spend on myself? Why did I get a positive spiritual vibe over buying books but not coffee? Eventually I put six dollars in a kitty for the food bank. Later that day I subtly got my co-worker to buy me a second cup so that I wouldn't have to repeat the experience.

It was more work than I expected to match everything I spent, and as the first week stretched on, my excitement began to wear off. The whole exercise was exhausting. Maybe fifty-fifty sharing would be easy for someone who only has two shirts and some spare food, but to share half of everything you have when you have so much requires a lot of planning and intentionality. (And yes, nothing had ever made me feel more privileged and spoiled than thinking, "It's so hard to share all of this stuff.")

I did not enjoy coming to terms with how often I purchased things. I think of "the consumer culture" as something I'm surrounded with more so than I consider myself a consumer. But by the end of the first week it became apparent that there probably wouldn't be a day's break in this exercise unless I locked myself in the house for the purpose of not spending money. I had no idea how spending had become such a mindless activity for me.

Despite my weariness with the whole thing, I spent some time thinking about the dentist appointments we had for the following week. I needed x-rays, which meant the bill would be higher than usual. I wondered whether I should research dental charities, or if God would bring someone with bad teeth across my path. I honestly had never spent any time before thinking about other people's mouths.

The next day, Sunday, I was browsing through the classifieds section of the newspaper when I saw an advertisement for an ministry that provides cleft palate surgeries for children whose families would never otherwise be able to afford it. I knew exactly how I would match our dentist bill. My family would get x-rays and clean teeth while some child in South America would have a life-changing operation at the same cost. It didn't seem fair that we had so much and they had so little. But in that moment, sharing the blessings I had felt like a joyful opportunity much more than a project. I wondered if God had divinely placed the advertisement just for me and my month-long project. But then I wondered if it had been in the newspaper often and I had just never "seen" it before. Was God giving me new opportunities, or was he giving me eyes to see the opportunities that had always been there?

The dentist bill was a breakthrough in the exercise, and for a while it almost seemed easy again. When I purchased thirty-two dollars worth of gas, I computed that the same amount would buy a bike for a family in India. When we spent over three hundred dollars on food, our family went on a shopping spree for the local food bank. The planning and intentionality and recording continued to be time consuming, but it was energy-giving, not energy-zapping.

As the month continued, I discovered what a difference it made in my heart when I prayed for the people I was giving to. I prayed for the plight of the Kenyan students living in slums; I prayed for the child who would be undergoing the cleft palate operation; I prayed for our stylist's client who had gone through bankruptcy and lost her business. I didn't even know the names of any of these people, but our lives were connected through the act of giving and receiving.

James 2:16 says, "If one of you says to them, 'Go in peace; keep warm and well fed,' but does nothing about their physical needs, what good is it?" James was correcting a kind of empty spiritualism that isn't backed up by action and real care. But it's also possible to swing to the other end, and to address someone's physical needs without concern for their heart and spirit. Either way, when we separate the physical and spiritual and elevate one over the other, we're not caring for the whole person. I felt something adjust and balance in my heart when I started praying as I gave.

Towards the end of the month, an unsettling realization occurred to me as I was tallying up all the money my family had spent on Christmas gifts. I prayed and asked God to bring to mind a local family that I could give six hundred dollars to for Christmas gifts—someone who wouldn't be able to afford Christmas gifts for their family. God didn't bring anyone to mind, so I prayed some more. Still nothing. I continued to wait for an answer until the truth finally settled in. *I didn't know any local poor families.* I traveled and ministered in impoverished places all over the world, but I didn't have a single poor friend in my own community. I was asking God to miraculously show me a poor family I could give money to; he was gently asking me why my life didn't already include them.

Some quick research on the matter said that I wasn't alone. Most people "stick to their kind" in terms of socio-economic status and levels of education. There are reasonable explanations for why this is the case. The people with whom our lives most naturally intersect (our neighbors and our colleagues) are typically in a similar income bracket as us. But there are other reasons why we don't cross class lines when choosing friends. *It's easier.* It doesn't challenge us to look beyond the surface differences of our lifestyles for deeper common ground.

All of these reasons make sense from a worldly perspective, where friendship is a commodity and poverty is a cause. But people were never a *cause* to Jesus, and they shouldn't be to me, either. I should have friends who are poor. I should be helping them and learning from them as they help me and learn from me. I should be sharing meals with them; we should be in each other's homes. I shouldn't need an organization to share my money with a family in need in my own community.

Over holiday dinners with our extended families, I looked across tables overflowing with food and abundance I realized how truly wealthy I am. One of the first lessons that God taught me over the month was not that I was greedy and materialistic, but that I was too far removed from the poor. I reconsidered John's command, and it started to sound like a mathematic word problem. *A man who has two shirts gives one shirt to a man who has no shirts. What's left? Two men, each with one shirt.* In the grand scheme of things, it is truly that simple. No one is saved and no one is made a hero when everyone is simply sharing.

As the month came to an end, I reflected on the journal I had kept and wrote down three insights from the exercise. I also identified three hang-ups that I encountered during the month...three things that I think often keep us from sharing as freely and generously as John invites us to share.

Insight One: Love and gratitude are the balance.

I spent much of my Christmas shopping thinking about the right "balance" in my spending. Money was flying out of my wallet faster than a tornado in Kansas, and it was leaving me dizzy. I wasn't thinking about how much I should be giving away in comparison to how much I spent—I was only thinking about how much I should have in the end. Even if I gave away half of everything that I kept, what should I be left with? And what about gifts? I love buying gifts for my wife and kids. What's the right balance when it comes to blessing my own family?

I thought about the balance that different friends of ours have struck when it comes to Christmas shopping. I know some families who give each other handmade gifts, which sounds horrible to me. I know other families who spend thousands of dollars on Christmas gifts for each other, which sounds excessive and wasteful to me. I wonder if people who spend more than me think I'm cheap and if those who spend less than me think I'm being extravagant. That's what's tough about seeking after "balance." How do you know if you've struck it, and who decides?

The conclusion I came to is that love and gratitude are better things to aim for than balance. They are the antidotes to selfishness and greed. "Trying to be more balanced" will have you looking at your feet all the time, trying not to trip. Who wants to spend their life simply trying not to fall over? Love and gratitude are better guides for handling money than trying to find a healthy balance in our isolated lives, or by comparing ourselves to others. Once you are connected to people you love, and once you view your things as a gift from God, sharing will come naturally.

Insight Two: Spending and giving are both spiritual exercises.

When we spend, we're receiving the gift of provision that God has given to us. When we give, we're sharing it with others. Both spending and giving are opportunities to worship.

When we were paying for our daughter's piano lessons, we asked her instructor about sponsoring a few lessons for someone. Her response was incredible. Instead of answering right away with the couple names that I'm sure were on the top of her head, she paused. Then she told us she wanted to pray seriously about whom to offer the piano lessons to. I was really impressed that she didn't treat our offer flippantly, but that she treated giving like a spiritual act of worship.

What if we treated all of our spending as a spiritual devotion?

What if we prayed before spending the way we pray before eating? Just the discipline itself would make us more mindful of our money and grateful for what we have, and the constant flow of prayer would open up so much space for the Holy Spirit to direct and guide us.

Insight Three: Giving isn't just about meeting someone else's needs; it's also about our character transformation.

People like to argue about whether or not we can ever be truly selfless when we give. Do we give because we want to feel good about ourselves? Do we give so that we won't feel guilty about what we have while others have not?

There are a couple reasons why I believe this question is the wrong focus. First, it carries an every-so-slight assumption that only wealthy people are in a position to share, when in truth, we are all called to share. John certainly wasn't talking to the rich when he said that a man with two shirts should give away one. Would we ask a man sharing his only bowl of rice if he's doing it to feel better about himself, or to alleviate his guilt over having rice? Does it matter to the hungry person he's sharing with?

Second, we're *supposed* to be affected by the act of giving. God designed us to be interdependent on each other, to rely on one another, to·give and to receive. If we think that giving should be an entirely selfless act that only changes and benefits the receiver, maybe we're forgetting just how needy we are as well. We need God's power to transform our hearts. We don't wait to give until our motivations to give are selfless and perfect, because it's through the act of giving that God begins to perfect our motivations.

And finally, giving to relieve guilt simply doesn't work. One of the lower points of the exercise was when my wife and I went shopping for Christmas dinner. As we were walking through the aisles buying all of the ingredients for a holiday feast, Marie told me how guilty she was feeling about the money we were spending on one meal. Was it too extravagant? Was it a waste of resources? I think it was *because* we had been giving so much that she was feeling guilty. She was feeling more in-tune with other people's needs and was suddenly more mindful about what we were spending on ourselves.

Guilt isn't good or bad; it's merely true or false. The question was whether buying food for a family holiday dinner should warrant guilt. Marie and I discussed how we needed to learn to live in grace. We needed to find a way to spend thoughtfully, give generously, and live with a sense of gratitude rather than guilt over the blessings we've been given.

The discipline of sharing does change us. It changes our perspective. When we share, we're choosing to turn our eyes outward, beyond our own needs and our own desires. Each of us has enough problems, hardships, responsibilities and goals to fill all of our own thoughts, all day, every day.

It's easy to get caught up in our leading roles and forget that we're a part of something much bigger. Sharing is like taking down one of the mirrors we live with and installing a window in its place.

So what keeps us from sharing? Is it self-worry and or greed, or are there other factors that keep us from being generous? As I thought through some of the questions and emotions I had encountered during the exercise, I arrived at three hang-ups that commonly hold us back from sharing freely.

Hang-up 1: People who want my money may not be deserving or trustworthy.

Who can we trust? How do we know our money will be handled appropriately? We've all heard stories of corrupt charities and ministry scams and beggars who actually live in nice homes. Examples like those make us untrusting and reluctant to get involved.

After she got a haircut, my daughter suggested that we look up charities that donate wigs to children with cancer. I went online to find one, and a few clicks later I was bombarded with a debate regarding the legitimacy of a particular charity. It bothered me thinking that—if the claims I was reading were true—an organization would take advantage of people with cancer and those who want to help them.

One day we went to deliver food to a food bank. People had driven there to receive free food, and I noticed a car in the food pick-up lane was much newer and nicer than mine. Was this someone who had enough money to buy food and who was taking resources from people who really needed food? Was this someone who couldn't afford to buy food because he purchased too nice of a car?

I realized that I was judging whether this stranger *deserved* the gift I was giving. How different my heart is from God's heart. I was trying to give an equal share to good people who were less fortunate than me. God gave his full share to us while we were guilty and dark with sin. Not one of us is worthy or deserving of the gifts God gives us, and yet we want to vet everyone who we share his gifts with. God blesses us knowing that we may squander his gifts or even do something damaging with them.

I'll still choose to give through charities that have integrity and I still want to give to people who legitimately need the resources I have to share. But the possibility of corruption, mishandling or misappropriation shouldn't keep us from giving.

If we make a mistake or our money ends up misused, we can remember that part of giving is about our character transformation and obedience, and that nothing is wasted in the process of obeying Jesus as best we can.

Hang-up 2: I'm embarrassed. I'm afraid I'll make things worse.

The first time that we donated to our local food bank, we went out and purchased the items ourselves. I had yet to do any research, and that was the only way I knew how to share food.

The first embarrassment I felt was that I had never before donated to our local food pantry. Donating for the first time made me realize about how negligent I had been in the past, and I didn't like the feeling. The other time I felt embarrassed was when I dropped off the food, and I had to carry the bags past people in line while their eyes were on me. I hated it. Not only did I feel uncomfortable, but I also wondered if walking by people in need with bags of food was reinforcing a mindset that marginalizes people who have less. I was suddenly worried that I was making a situation worse in my eagerness to be helpful.

The question of responsible giving and how to help people without disempowering them is an important one. But no matter how researched and smart we are in the matter of giving, we are probably going to make some mistakes along the way. The important thing is that we don't throw our hands up and say, "Well then I won't even bother." Helping people can be a difficult, complicated and even painful thing to enter into, but opting out isn't the answer. We need to be willing to engage the mess.

Hang-up 3: Someone else needs to be responsible. I can't make a big enough difference.

Paying for the cleft palate surgery was one of the most satisfying gifts that we gave during our month-long exercise. To know that we could change the life of a child with a single donation was a joy and a privilege. But after making the donation, I felt a new burden for kids in need of cleft palate operations. I was tempted to research how many there are in the world, but I knew the statistic would depress me, so I didn't look it up.

It's easy to get angry about the extreme injustices in the world. It's easy to get angry at the unfair global distribution system where one child gets regular teeth cleanings and another is stuck with no options in life. What's difficult is coming to terms with the fact that we are the unjust global distribution system—that all of us together make it up. There is no "they" out there who is ultimately responsible. We each have an equal responsibility to do what we can with the resources we have.

Feeling that sense of responsibility is overwhelming. Our culture is very task-oriented, and task-oriented people don't like to take on something that they can't complete. We like a project we can conquer and solve; and "help those in need" isn't something we can check off a list. We need to let go of our desire to *solve* and be willing to simply *share*.

A Sharing Lifestyle

Sharing is not a month-long project or an exercise. Sharing is a lifestyle. It's helping those whom God puts across our path. It's listening to the voice of the Holy Spirit when God puts a particular person or cause or opportunity on our hearts. It's structuring our mindsets and our finances so that we have the freedom to give, no matter what our income. It's choosing to open our death grips on stuff and start working the word "mine" out of our vocabularies. Want to see your stuff different? Want to cultivate a new sense of gratitude? Sometimes we have to try something different in order to gain a different perspective. You could pick a particular category of your spending and match it, or you could make it a point to give creatively to a new person every week. There are lots of different ways that you could go about it, but simply taking the leap on whatever comes to your mind is a great first step. Whether or not it was God who directed me to this exercise in the first place, he certainly used it to wake me up. I didn't end the month with easy answers to a complicated, messy topic of wealth and sharing. If anything, I came out of it with more questions than I started with. But there was one thing I knew for certain: I never wanted see my stuff the same way again.

Life Application

1. How do you see your stuff – as belonging to you, or as belonging to God and to be shared?

2. Do you see yourself as a giver or as a sharer and how does that difference matter?

3. What would be the most daunting part of undergoing a fifty-fifty sharing exercise like this?

4. Which of the "hang-ups" did you most identify with? What keeps you from sharing freely?

5. If you could change one thing about how you manage your stuff, what would it be?

Joel Holm

Chapter Five

Time

There is a time for everything, and a season for every activity under heaven; a time to be born, and a time to die, a time to plant and a time to uproot, a time to kill and a time to heal, a time to tear down and a time to build, a time to weep and a time to laugh, a time to mourn, and a time to dance.

Ecclesiastes 3:1-4

You've heard the phrase, "Live every day like it's your last." This modern proverb is thrown around so frequently that we typically don't bother to examine it. It sounds fine, even if it is impossible to follow for those of us who have jobs and responsibilities. (Who would unload the dishwasher or finish a work report on the last day of his life?) But other than that, it sounds inspiring! Squint, and it almost looks like a mash-up of some of our favorite Jesus quotes: "I have come so that you may have life and have it to the full" and "Why do you worry about tomorrow? Tomorrow will take care of itself."

But what's the assumption behind this cliché piece of advice? "Live every day like it's your last" assumes that only thing we have in life is the present moment. If there's no bigger story to your life than what you feel and experience in the present moment, then the best you can do is be happy and make the most of right here, right now.

But the full life that Jesus came to offer us looks different than simply finding whatever happiness we can find today. We need a greater context for our individual moments. In order to live a day well, we need a sense of how that day fits into the bigger picture.

God designed us to live seasonally. Like nature, our lives pass through various seasons for the purpose of growth. Each season looks different, feels different, and serves a different purpose. A well-lived day in one season looks different than a well-lived day in another, and we need to understand and embrace the various stages of our lives in order to embrace God's purpose, blessing and abundance. To rewrite that bit of pop wisdom, we should *live every day intentionally, according to the season it belongs to.*

When we live with a day-to-day mindset instead of the bigger picture, whatever is happening at that moment becomes "everything." When times are bad, we get discouraged and lose hope that life will ever be joyful again. When times are good, we take life for granted and don't prepare or brace for difficult seasons on the horizon. Having a seasonal outlook on life doesn't mean that you won't experience the emotions of whatever season you're in: discouragement, sadness, frustration, excitement, joy, and so on. But you'll experience those emotions without the despair or false hope that your current stage of life will last forever. You'll be able to endure it, enjoy it, learn from it and live it well… for exactly what it is, when it is.

Jesus lived his life intentionally in seasons. He did this by being in tune with the season that his Father had him in, and then by protecting that season for what it was. First he lived in a season of preparation, which he spent learning and identifying his purpose. In his wilderness season, he completely isolated himself and practiced being dependent on the Father. There were seasons of his ministry that were for multitudes and teaching and miracles and traveling, while other seasons were about laying low and pouring into his disciples. Jesus was clear about the purpose of each season, and he didn't let opportunities or outside pressures distract him from what that season was about.

Identifying your season

The first layer to identifying your season is to identify the stage of life you're in. This is pretty easy. Just look at your age, family, relationships, what you do, and the purpose for which you do it. Are you twenty-something and starting a career? You're in a season of learning, discovering and defining. Are you newly married? You're in a season of building a foundation for your marriage and future. Are you thirty-five with young kids? You're in a season of nurturing and giving. Are you an empty nester? You are reaping a harvest while sowing new seeds for the second half of your life. Are you starting a new business? Are you taking care of an ailing parent? Are you welcoming grandchildren? Retiring? Well into old age? Each of these stages comes with a different purpose and a different blueprint for abundant daily life.

Not every season falls into neat categories like these. Maybe you're fifty and just starting a marriage or new career, or maybe you're twenty-five and widowed. The most difficult and confusing seasons are often the ones that take us by surprise, or that don't fit into the mold of what life was "supposed" to look like. Some seasons are as predictable as spring in Chicago. *It's snowing? It was sixty degrees last Saturday!* It might take a little more reflection and creativity to name the stage you're in if it doesn't fit a standard mold, so get creative and reflective! After you've named your season of life, consider your current spiritual season.

A spiritual season is something independent of a life stage, and we can find ourselves in any one of these spiritual seasons no matter where we are in life. There's the *wilderness season,* where no matter how hard we pray it feels like we're banging against a brick wall. There are *seasons of hunger and thirsting,* where it takes no effort to pray, read the Bible and passionately seek the Lord, because the desire is overflowing out of our hearts. There are *seasons of worship,* where we're drawn to music and nature and feel a sense of wonder and awe. Most Christians go through *seasons of doubt,* where we question God or his goodness. There are *seasons of attack,* where every day brings another fire to put out, and problems pile up until we feel weak and beaten down. There are also *seasons of overwhelm*, which is not so much about problems as it is the intense demands on our time and energy. All of us delight in *seasons of joy*, where God feels near and we live with a sense of joy and purpose.

Our individual lives happen in the context of family, community, society and the greater world. Each of the spheres also goes through seasons that will affect us, and it's important to be thoughtful about them. Marriages move through various stages based on where each partner is in life and how their desires, goals and needs combine at a particular time. Families go through seasons based what's happening in the family (a move, a new job, a new baby, etc.) and on the age of kids—the young childhood years, the teenage years, the college years, the empty nester years. Too often parents recognize the seasons in parenting only in hindsight, after their kids are out of the house. Time passes fast, but it goes even faster when we're not making the most of the season.

Extended families go through seasons as well. There may be times in your life where your extended family is just humming along in the background, requiring nothing more than some phone calls and messages and planning for get-togethers. Other times there's an illnesses or a death that suddenly requires a lot more of your time, energy and attention. If you recognize new seasons as they arrive, you'll be more emotionally equipped to face the challenge thoughtfully, intentionally and healthfully.

If you've been part of one church for any length of time, then you know churches go through seasons. So many people join or leave churches based on the current state of the church. Rather than seeing a church's movement in phases, stages and seasons, it's easy to think that the church simply "is" whatever happened on a particular Sunday morning or over the course of a few months. But if you're on board with a church's overall heart and mission, then you can weather its various seasons and be a part of its long-term story.

Our culture and society goes through seasons. Western cultures in particular are very self-aware (or perhaps self-focused) about defining and critiquing our various stages as a culture. And beyond our culture, we experience global seasons.

Right now we're in an era of globalization, where the world is becoming more and more connected through transportation and communication technologies. If we're going to "Live wisely among non-Christians and make the most of every opportunity," (Colossians 4:5), then we need to be aware of our place and role in society and the global community. We belong to a specific point in history, and that we're here on earth at this particular time for a purpose.

Understanding the seasons that your family, community, church, society and global community are currently in will further help you pinpoint your current season of life.

Living Intentionally in Your Season

Once you've identified your season, you have two good options: embrace the season you're in, or—if it's in your power and if it's how God is directing you—change it. Seasons pass without our "doing" anything about it, simply because time moves and life changes. But other times we stay stuck in a stage of life simply because we don't want to move forward. We're not willing to put the time and effort into our spiritual development, or we're too scared to take a risk, or we ignore a calling or an assignment. Naming the season you're in may help you identify how it needs to change.

One of the biggest mistakes you can make in changing your season is to do it out of a desire to escape your current season, or because you don't fully trust what God has for you in your current season. For example, be careful not to marry someone simply because you don't want to be single anymore; instead, exhaust your single season and move into marriage when you've met the person that you want to love and serve for the rest of your life. Don't change jobs or move to another state just because you're bored or stir crazy or want to escape something. If you're bored and stir crazy, ask God for vision and purpose. Maybe he'll reveal a vision and purpose that requires a job change and relocation, or maybe he'll give you a vision and purpose right where you are. The point is, don't expect that by forcibly moving into another season of life, you're going to change or solve any deeper heart issues that are unresolved in your current season.

Naming the season you're in may be the first step toward changing your season, once you've determined that the change is not for the sake of escape, and once you're sure that you have exhausted everything God has for you in your current season. Or, naming the season you're in may be the first step toward consciously accepting and embracing it. Even if it's hard. Even if it's not as good as the last season you were in or one you hope to be in. Even if it's a season of doubt or wilderness or a stage of life that you find challenging and disappointing.

The Christian journey is often described as a race. Paul, of course, describes it as such when he writes, "I press on in the race before me, straining…" Usually we read that verse and picture a sprint or a marathon, with a runner putting one foot in front of the other and straining at an even pace. I prefer to picture an obstacle course, and each new season of life as a new obstacle to work through. Some are especially fun and some are especially difficult. Some of them capitalize on our natural talents while others come with a learning curve. Some we move through quickly and with ease, while others we have to spend more time fumbling and stumbling through.

But they're all part of the same course, and each one is moving us closer to the prize.

When my father was diagnosed with cancer, we immediately came together as a family to pray. My father is someone who understands that life passes through good times and difficult times, and that every stage is a chance to go further into the life that God has for him. He prayed, *God, whatever you're going to take me through, would you fully invade my life so that I can be used by you? Would your abundance, blessing and presence fill me in this season of life, whatever it may be?* Like many seasons, cancer isn't something you can opt out of; it's only something you can walk through. Knowing the season you're in and accepting it means you can start asking the questions that will lead to fuller life right here, right now, in the exact season you're in. But if we go through life without the full obstacle course in mind, our tendency is to resist the difficult seasons.

Here are some the symptoms of season resistance: You say "yes" to things you should say "no" to, and vice versa. You look for more options to escape your season and stage of life rather than to support it. You feel like you're in "survival mode," just waiting to get to the next thing, content if you make it to bed at night in one piece. You rarely, if ever, end your day with a sense of accomplishment, purpose and satisfaction with how you spent your time. You aren't being authentic with yourself and others about your spiritual state.

When we know, accept and embrace the season of life that we're in, it's easier to focus our time and energy. We intuitively know which things to say "yes" and "no" to. Living seasonally means we can even say "no" to good things because we're clear what belongs in our current season and what does not.

For a while my wife and I went through a particularly stressful season in our finances. Despite all of our attempts to be obedient in giving and wise with our spending, we were barely making bills. Our first reaction was to resist and question the season. *God, why are you allowing this to happen? Don't you see how much stress we're under? Don't you want us to be happy and blessed?* With that initial reaction came a desire to immediately escape or resolve the season, even if it wasn't a long-term solution. *Maybe we can borrow money from our families. Maybe we can cut back on our giving.* Finally, through prayer and reflection, we arrived at a place of acceptance. *OK, God, even though we don't understand the purpose of this season, we're going to trust that you're working in it. What do you want to teach us? How do you want us to walk through it?* We discovered that we were in a season of faith development. We learned to depend on God's faithfulness in new ways.

A friend of mine experienced a season completely opposite when he was left a large sum of money and went from scraping-by to wealthy overnight. Sometimes we only think to turn to the Lord in a season that feels difficult and out of our control, but my friend acknowledged that he needed God in his season of blessing as well. He asked similar questions. *God, why did you do this? What's your purpose in it? How do you want me to walk through it?*

It's tempting to compare seasons with other people. We look up from our difficult obstacle and see someone else flying through his or her current obstacle with ease. While I was going through a wilderness season, a friend of mine was going through a season of hunger and thirsting. I had absolutely no motivation to read the Bible; he was reading the Bible from five till nine every morning. I thought maybe I could escape my season by doing what he was doing in his. Not surprisingly, I found myself putting in a lot of time and effort and yielding very little result. Rather than try to force my way into a different season, I should have asked the Lord: *How can I pursue spiritual growth in the season that you have me in? What do you want to teach me in it?* The dry spell didn't last forever and I was able to see the purpose in it—but that was despite my effort to escape it.

God is the Orchestrator of Seasons

Whether you can live in each season with a sense of peace and purpose ultimately boils down to the question of trust. Do you believe that God loves you and is trustworthy? Do you believe that the seasons and stages of your life serve a purpose? Do you believe that your life belongs to a greater story? If you do, then you can live without anxiety for tomorrow or the next season of your life, and you can focus instead on making the most of the current day and the season God has you in right now.

Seasonal living is really the only way to make the most of the present day. You can live right here, right now—not looking behind you and wishing for what was, and not trying to escape your present season for something better ahead. The past is gone and the next will come; today is gift that you can only fully appreciate in the context of seasons.

But there's an even greater purpose to seasonal living than getting the most out of our lives as we can. The greatest purpose of the seasons in our lives is *to discover who God is.* God reveals himself to us through planting and uprooting, laughing and mourning, tearing and building. He doesn't just want to show us the way; he wants to show us who he is. Because it's in him—not our plans, not our destiny, not anything that we do or become— that we find peace, joy and satisfaction. Want to see your time different? Want to break free from the impossible pressure to live like you're dying tomorrow and start living fully and intentionally, according to the season you're in? There's no place to start except in the exact season you're in, right now.

Life Application

Here are some questions to journal or reflect on. Spending some time answering these questions should give you a pretty clear picture of what season you're in, which will provide you with clarity and direction on how you can be living your fullest life right now.

1. What stage of life am I in? When did this stage begin? Approximately how long do I think it will last?

2. Of the following, which best describes my spiritual state: wilderness, hunger and thirsting, worship, doubt, attack, overwhelm, or joy? How long have I been in this spiritual state? What purpose might there be in it?

3. What season of life are the members of my family in?

4. What season is my place of work currently in?

5. What stage is my church in? What direction is it going?

6. What domestic or world events are taking place right now? How am I ready to be salt and light?

7. What activities and forms of relaxation would best support and enhance this season?

Chapter Six

Faith

Overhearing what they said, Jesus told him, "Don't be afraid; just believe."

Mark 5:36

What does it mean to live courageously?

A few years ago I dropped my wife off in front of a restaurant in downtown Chicago and went to park the car. I was walking across the street to join her when, out of the corner of my eye, I saw a fairly large man running directly toward her. Before I realized what was happening, he body slammed her to the ground, took her purse, and ran. I rushed over to her, calling, "Marie! Are you okay?" She stood up on her own and said, "Yeah, I'm fine." I quickly looked her over to make sure she was really okay. Then I took off running.

I was running after a thief in downtown Chicago when I heard my wife yelling my name, so I glanced back and saw *her* running after *me*. It was like a slapstick routine that was going to end with a three-way collision. I was yelling, "STOP! Thief! Drop my wife's purse!" She was yelling, "STOP! Joel! You're an idiot! He may have a gun!"

I kept running, but my thoughts started to catch up with my legs. *So, what if I get to him? What am I going to do? I don't exactly ooze intimidation. Really, what am I going to do? Hand him my wallet and say, "You forgot this"?*

I knew exactly what would happen if the guy turned around and came toward me. I would turn around and start running toward my wife! But to my surprise, the thief dropped my wife's purse and ran away.

A few days later I was telling this story to a friend. I was exaggerating, just a little...about minor details like the thief's size and how brave I was to chase him. I finished the story and my friend said, "Wow, Joel. You were really

See. Life. Different.

courageous." My wife, who happened to be standing there, quickly replied with a grin on her face, "No. Joel wasn't courageous. Just dumb."

The jury is still out between us on whether I was brave or dumb on that day. What I learned from the experience was that when I suffered a personal injustice, such as someone attacking my wife, it was very instinctual for me to take a risk and put myself in danger. But when it comes living out my faith—to proclaiming the name of Jesus and following the call he's put on my life—it isn't always that instinctual. How could my "fight" instinct be so strong when it came to defending my wife, when so often I feel a "flight" instinct when it comes to defending Jesus or to following him out to the end of a limb?

I think we often have a wrong idea of what it means to be courageous, to have a great faith. We only see the end point of faith and not the starting point. But we are called to live a life of faith, so its important to know where that faith begins. The Bible gives us a short account of a man named Nicodemus, a Pharisee. Nicodemus isn't the first person we think of when it comes to brave characters in the Bible, but I think his story tells us a lot about becoming a person of courage. The first time we're introduced to Nicodemus is in John 3.

> *John 3:1-2: Now there was a Pharisee, a man named Nicodemus who was a member of the ruling Jewish council. He came to Jesus at night and said, "Rabbi, we know you are a teacher who has come from God. For no one could perform the signs you are doing if God was not with him."*

What's so bold about sneaking out to meet Jesus in the dark of the night, when no one could see him? Nothing. Being a courageous person of faith does not start with an act of bravery. It starts with what I call "holy dissatisfaction."

Holy dissatisfaction is the feeling in your gut that there has to be something more than what you currently have or experience. Nicodemus was a person who had reached an apex of spirituality. He was someone other people went to with their questions about faith. But he knew in his gut that there was something more, and that there was something to this Jesus he had encountered. Even though he wasn't brave enough to approach Jesus during the day, he was humble enough to go to him at night.

In what area of your life do you feel a sense of "holy dissatisfaction"? Is there a dream you believe God gave you that hasn't come to pass? Are you stalled in an area where you thought you'd be further along? Nicodemus was discontent because he realized that maybe the answers he had to life weren't the right answers. Maybe there was something else.

When you find yourself living with this kind of righteous angst, you have one of two choices to make. First, you could build fence around your dissatisfaction and avoid it completely. Nicodemus could have done this by looking around and realizing that he was the only Pharisee in his crowd with a question for Jesus, while the rest of them were all falling in line around the same answers. *Maybe I'm wrong to have this question,* he could have thought. *Maybe I was wrong about that dream,* we might think. *Maybe I'm wrong to think I should be living differently. Maybe everything is fine just as it is.*

Or you could do something else—something between giving up and a brave leap. After acknowledging your discontentment, you could ask an honest question. An honest question is, quite simply, a question that you honestly don't know the answer to. (If you already have the answer, you don't honestly have a question; what you have is an answer that you want God to bless.)

To ask an honest question, you have to acknowledge your weakness. When you look at the people who approached Jesus during his ministry, you'll see that most of them came not in strength, but in weakness. They came broken and in despair. They came needing hope and healing. They came with honest questions.

Marie and I were friends with a young married couple with three little kids, and one day Marie got a call from the wife, sobbing. "My husband found another woman," she said. "He ran away. He just left." The aftermath in the following weeks and months was brutal, but what made it even worse were the well-meaning people who kept telling her, "You need to be strong. You need to persevere. Just hang in there!"

One night Marie and I went over to this woman's house for dinner, and I knew I had a word for her. I said, "I think I have something God wants me to share with you. I think he wants you to know that you can be weak right now. You can go to him with empty hands. You can go to him with questions. The only thing you need the courage to do is to bring your weakness to him."

That's where it starts. Being weak in your own strength will get you nowhere, but if you bring your weakness to Christ, his power can be made perfect in it. If you bring your honest question to God rather than the answer you want him to deliver—that's the start of faith.

Oftentimes we come to God because we want his plan for our lives. If he'll only give us *the plan*, then we can be courageous about it. But being a courageous person of faith doesn't revolve around a plan; it revolves around a person, Jesus. Nicodemus went to Jesus because he was drawn to him and he needed to know who he was. And it was in that private conversation with Nicodemus—not in a synagogue and not on a hilltop—that Jesus revealed the great plan.

> *For God so loved the world, that he gave his one and only Son, that whosoever believes in him shall not perish but have eternal life. For God did not send his Son into the world to condemn the world, but to save the world through him. (John 3:16)*

I've ministered in ninety-two countries. When people hear that number, they often say, "You must really have a heart for missions, Joel." No, not particularly. I just love Jesus, and when I centered my life on him, I somehow ended up in ninety-two countries. When other people center their lives on him, he leads them to do all sorts of other things. But it starts by going to him with an honest question. *Who are you? Will you show yourself to me?*

A while after Nicodemus goes to Jesus in the dark of the night, the Pharisees want to see Jesus arrested and killed. Nicodemus finds himself in the middle of this great controversy.

Finally the temple guards went back to the chief priests and the Pharisees, who asked them, "Why didn't you bring him in?" "No one ever spoke the way this man does," the guards replied. "You mean he has deceived you also?" the Pharisees retorted. "Have any of the rulers or the Pharisees believed in him? No! But this mob that knows nothing of the law—there is a curse on them." (John 7:45-49)

Nicodemus is there during this confrontation between the guards and the Pharisees, and he's listening as the Pharisees scoff that no one with a serious understanding of the law has comes to the conclusion that Jesus is for real. What does Nicodemus do?

Nicodemus, who had gone to Jesus earlier and who was one of their own number, asked, "Does our law condemn a man without first hearing him to find out what he has been doing?" They replied, "Are you from Galilee, too? Look into it and you'll find that a prophet does not come out of Galilee." (John 7:50-51)

Nicodemus defended Jesus and he got flak for it. He didn't have to defend Jesus. Jesus wasn't even there to hear him! This was a man who, a few months before, had snuck out in the middle of the night because he was too cowardly be seen with Jesus. Now it's the light of day in an intense situation, and he's defending him. What happened?

When I was about twenty, I was working my way through college and serving in a church. I found myself discouraged with the fact that while it was easy for me to preach and share about Jesus within the church walls, every time I went out into the world, I would clam up and let opportunities pass. It started to weigh me down a lot, but the guilt was never motivating enough to overcome my self-consciousness and fear.

Around that same time, I asked my wife to marry me. Honestly, it was a coin toss whether she was going to say yes or not. I knew we loved each other, but I didn't have very much to offer her at that point in my life. Still, I worked up the courage to go to her apartment with a ring in my pocket, and I got down on my knee, still convinced she was going to say no. I asked, "Will you marry me?" She said, "Yes."

"No," I said. "You don't understand. Will you spend the rest of your life with me?"

"Yes," she said.

"No, you must not get it. I have nothing to offer you."

She said, "Joel, I'll give you the rest of my life."

When I left her apartment, I was dancing to the elevator. The door closed and I found myself alone with a total stranger. "She said yes!" I told the stranger. He didn't ask, but I told him the whole story. We landed in the lobby and the doorman held open the door for me. "She said YES!" I told the doorman, and then I told him the whole story, too.

I honestly could not have cared less what anyone thought as I went through my day proclaiming, "She said yes!" Maybe a few people thought I was an idiot, but I was simply too overcome with happiness and love to care.

1 John 4:18 says, "There is no fear in love. But perfect love casts out all fear."

Love is the center of courage. Guilt, obligation and duty can modify behavior, but only love can motivate true courage. Typically we read 1 John 4:18 and think that it's the love that Jesus has for us that casts out our fear. But I think it's the love we have for him *in response to his love for us* that truly motivates courage. When you're afraid, your eyes are on yourself—on your fears, your concerns, and your anxieties. When you love, your eyes are off yourself and on the object of your love. The fear for yourself is gone because you're not even looking at it. I've met courageous Christians all over the world who have risked their lives out of faithful obedience to Jesus, and all of them were motivated by one thing: love for Jesus.

Peter had a moment to be courageous, and he blew it. When the rooster crowed three times and he realized what he had done, he was tormented by it. I think most of us feel sorry for Peter when we read this passage, because we know how Peter feels. Would we also have failed? Would we have had courage in that dark moment? In other ways, we know we have done just what Peter did. But when Jesus first regroups with Peter, he doesn't ask him, "Peter, are you really sorry? Peter, are you going to do better next time?" He doesn't ask, "Peter, will you get your act together?" Instead he asks, "Peter, do you love me?" Jesus was getting ready to call Peter into his ministry as an apostle—a calling that would eventually cost him his life. Peter's future would require far more boldness than the little he had just *proven* he didn't have. Jesus brought him back to the core of the matter: Peter, do you love me? Love would be the only thing to compel Peter into the courageous life he was chosen for. The last we hear about Nicodemus is in John 19:38-40.

Later, Joseph of Arimathea asked Pilate for the body of Jesus. Now Joseph was a disciple of Christ, but secretly, because he feared the Jewish leaders. With Pilate's permission, he came and took the body away. He was accompanied by Nicodemus, the man who earlier had visited Jesus at night. Nicodemus brought a mixture of myrrh and aloes, about seventy-five pounds. Taking Jesus' body, the two of them wrapped it, with the spices, in strips of linen. This was in accordance with the Jewish burial customs.

When we think of great acts of courage in the Bible, we think of Caleb and Joshua bringing back their report from the promise land, or David slaying Goliath, or Daniel in the lions' den. But among all these heroes of faith, we have this short story of a man named Nicodemus. He first sneaks away in the middle of the night with his burning question: *who are you?* He then defends Jesus among his group of religious rulers: *doesn't our law require that we give him a chance to speak?* And then we find him taking on the role of a servant, dressing the body of Jesus, offering what was likely his personal savings of burial spices.

I wonder what Nicodemus was thinking as he pried the nails out of Jesus' hands. Was he remembering the words Jesus spoke to him? *There's no condemnation here, Nicodemus, only love.* I wonder what was going through his mind as he defiled himself during the holy Passover week to dress a deceased body. Why would he do it? Jesus was dead. As far as Nicodemus knew, this was the end of the story.

Matthew 13 says that the Kingdom is like a priceless treasure hidden in a field, and when you find it, you sell everything to buy it. Courageous living is being so devoted to Jesus that you don't even think twice about giving up the small treasures you hold in your hand.

When my daughter was about four, the two of us were walking along a river when she suddenly fell in. I didn't bother to check the current, and I didn't take time to consider the temperature or danger. What parent would? I immediately jumped into the river to pull her out. I was so consumed with love and devotion for her that I literally had no concern for my life. Later that day as I was recounting the experience in my mind, I wondered if I would have been so immediate in my response if it had been a stranger's daughter who fell into the river. Real faith, real courage, is centered in a love for the person. Regardless of any circumstance, you will do whatever is needed.

I had one of the scariest flying experiences of my life a few years ago. I was flying in Siberia on a Russian airline, and with forty minutes left in the flight, the plane took a complete nosedive. People were screaming and bags were flying throughout the cabin when, suddenly, it leveled off. The dive felt like an eternity but probably only lasted about fifteen seconds. The pilot never explained what happened, and no one spoke for the rest of the flight. In that silence, I'll tell you what thought didn't cross my mind. "For me to live is Christ and to die is gain." Nope, it didn't cross my mind once! I just gripped the sides of my chair and made it through the rest of the flight.

I'm not quite where Nicodemus had grown to with Jesus, but I want to be. I want to be so consumed with love and devotion for him that my very life feels like a small thing to give up in comparison to the treasure that I've found in him.

Why did Nicodemus choose to care for Jesus' body? There were other things he could have done. He could have brought food to the disciples or

Jesus' mother, or he could have gone to the synagogue to pray. Why did he go to the cross? Nicodemus had the faith to go to the darkest place and provide all that he could. We need to be courageous in the very situation where we're waiting for God to show up. We may not be able to control the outcome of that situation, and our act of faith may seem insignificant. But what matters is that we offer it. *A phone call to extend grace to someone who has betrayed us. An offer to give the marriage another chance. A gift in the midst of financial hardship. A prayer for healing in the last hours.*

Don't try to be falsely courageous. Follow the way of Nicodemus. First, go to Jesus in your weakness. Second, find that moment when you will stand up for him as a first act of faith. And finally you will discover yourself so greatly in love with Jesus, that no matter where he leads you, you will follow.

Life Application

1. What area of weakness do you currently have that you need to bring to Jesus?

2. What's an honest question you can ask Jesus?

3. How can you make a stand, in faith, for Jesus, like Nicodemus did?

4. How have you seen your growing love for Jesus impact your faith and courage?

Joel Holm

Chapter Seven

Future

"For I know my plans for you, says the Lord. Plans to prosper and not to harm you. Plans to give you a hope and a future."

Jeremiah 29:11

Jeremiah 29:11 is one of the Bible's all-time greatest hits. Typically we see it in isolation (like it's quoted here), and most often it's presented as a promise. No matter what is wrong in our lives and no matter what darkness we face, Jeremiah 29:11 reminds us that God has a good plan for our lives.

While we tend to read the "you" in this passage as singular—that God has good plans for my individual life and your individual life—God gave this message to a whole community, the people of Israel, who were about to be taken from Jerusalem and exiled in Babylon. The "you" referred to his people, and he gave them this assurance following some specific instructions for *how* he wanted them to live in exile. God was telling his people that because his heart was to prosper and not to harm them, they could trust that his instructions were the best way to live.

A couple years ago my family relocated to a new community. As part of the moving process, we asked ourselves, "Now that we live here, *how* are we going to live here? What does our future look like in this community? How are we going to interact with our neighbors?" While there's certainly a world of difference between being forced into exile and relocating from one city to another, the questions we were asking were similar to the questions the Israelites faced when they arrived in Babylon.

And in a larger, spiritual sense, exile is actually a good picture of our life here on earth. We belong to the city of God and yet we're living in the city of man. Every day we live in the clash between kingdom culture and our modern secular culture, leaving us with a sense that we don't quite fit in and we don't fully belong. As Christians we realize we're living in a fallen world that's out of sync with what God created, but I think even non-Christians feel the angst of exile.

Our society is incredibly fragmented. People with a conservative bent think the world is becoming frighteningly liberal, and people with a liberal bent are scared the world is becoming increasingly conservative. Younger people feel like no one understands them and elderly people feel there's no place for them. The wealthy feel taken advantage of, the middle-class feels overlooked, and the poor feel like no one cares. Even in culturally diverse America, it's not uncommon to hear racial minorities express, "This isn't really my home. I don't belong here, not really." Sin fragments and divides, and it affects all of us. As Christians we can acknowledge this and then ask the next question. *How* are we going to live in exile? How are we going to live in this home that's not truly our home?

The Israelites had three options for how they would live in Babylon. Two of them were wrong and one was God's way. We see them laid out in Jeremiah 29:1-11.

> *This is what the Lord Almighty, the God of Israel, says to all those who I carried into exile from Jerusalem to Babylon. "Build houses and settle down; plant gardens and eat what they produce. Marry and have sons and daughters; find wives for your sons and give your daughters in marriage, so that they too may have sons and daughters. Increase in number there; do not decrease. Also, seek the peace and prosperity of the city to which I have carried you into exile. Pray to the Lord for it, because if it prospers, you too will prosper." Yes, this is what the Lord Almighty, the God of Israel, says: "Do not let the prophets and diviners among you deceive you. Do not listen to the dreams you encourage them to have. They are prophesying lies to you in my name. I have not sent them,"*

declares the Lord. "For I know the plans I have for you," declares the Lord.
"Plans to prosper and not to harm you. Plans to give you a hope and a future."

When it comes to how we are going to live in our communities and in this world, there are three ways that we can try to arrive at God's best for us. But only one of them is actually his best way for us to live.

Our first option is to become like the world.

In an attempt to fix the angst within us, we can act like this isn't exile at all. Maybe this is home. Maybe the best way to live is to stop thinking that there's something better, to forget Jerusalem, and to start living like this is the best there is. Maybe we should fit in and get the most out of this place as we possibly can.

Babylon was a powerful empire that had tried and tested a few different ways to deal with conquered people groups. First they tried banishment. The problem with banishment is that people tended to band together and come back with a fight. So then they tried oppressing the people they had conquered. The problem with oppression is that if you hold people down long enough, they try to rise up, and sometimes they succeed. Then Babylon tried a third way. They *welcomed* the people they conquered.

This is what Babylon did with the Israelites. They said, "Come join us. Be like us. Here, we'll even give you good jobs." The incentive and pressure to join Babylon was intense, but once you joined Babylon, you lost your identity. This was the conflict that Daniel, one of the central biblical figures of this time, faced. He was offered a high position and a bright future in

Babylon, but it was offered at the cost of his identity. To be accepted into Babylon, you had to bow to the empire. The goal was that the conquered people would decrease in power and identity and become an indistinguishable part of the community.

Sometimes we're tempted to go to the way of Babylon. In our modern Western society, I think the idol we're constantly being asked to bow down to is "relative truth." *If it works for you, do it. There's no one true religion. Keep your faith to yourself. Pray in your own home, but don't go near the window.* If you bow to these ideas, then you're considered a tolerant and enlightened person, which is the mark of belonging in our Babylon. The easiest way to live in our culture today is to concede that Christ is just one of the ways to God, and to practice "our" truth in the privacy of our own homes and churches.

The Israelites were tempted to go the way of Babylon—to decrease, to bow, and to fit in. Perhaps that was the way to get the best out of their lives and future. But God told them instead to increase, not to blend in and disappear as part of the overall society. They were to stand out. *Increase in number, do not decrease,* he said. *Plant a garden and make this home, but don't think I'm not coming back for you. Don't mistake this for your true home.*

Our second option is to keep the moving boxes packed.

This was the way of the Jewish leaders that God warned about. In chapter 28 we read of a false prophet who was telling people that they should resist Babylon and hold on, because God was coming back for them in two short years. Forget about building houses. Forget about making a life here. God's coming! We're out of here! Exploit Babylon for everything you need out of it, but don't put down roots or invest in it.

I met a Christian a while ago who told me he was moving to Idaho. When I asked what he was moving to Idaho for, he answered, "I'm sick of this city. I'm sick of the corruption and noise and pollution, so I'm moving to Idaho and I'm getting a cabin in the woods."

We can build a cabin in the woods no matter where we live. We can stay in our homes and the homes of a few good Christian friends; we can get out of society everything that we need from it—infrastructure, money and resources—but invest nothing in return. We can stay cocooned in our little Christian lives, just waiting out the exile.

One of the symptoms of "cabin living" is if you have no unbelieving friends. You surround yourself with only Christian people and Christian institutions. It's a way of hiding out and just waiting for God to bring in the future. Another symptom is if your primary interaction with the world is the war you're at with it. There are so many things I don't like about the world around me, and sometimes I want to retreat to the woods rather than deal with it. I don't like how the immorality we're constantly being bombarded with makes it harder for me to raise my children, and I don't like hearing my Lord and Savior mocked in public discourse and entertainment. It would be easy to move into a cabin in the woods and only venture out to do battle with the world's culture and values. But if I do that, then I'm removing myself from the very people whom God has called me to love.

Left to our own devices, these first two options are the only ones we come up with. *Join in, or reject.* Is this what my future is supposed to look like?

What other option is there?

God gives his people a third way, which is to seek the peace and prosperity of Babylon.

God tells the Israelites to play a role in determining His future for all people. He tells them to pray for it. After being ripped from their homes and taken captive, the Israelites probably wouldn't have thought to seek the peace and prosperity of their enemy. And it's not how we naturally go about interacting with our communities, either. Typically we look to our city to provide *us* with peace and prosperity. We want society to get its politics, infrastructure and economy in order so that we can live peaceful and prosperous lives. But God's instructions suggest that we actually have power in the situation. We have the grace; we have the light. *We* should be seeking the city's peace and prosperity, not the other way around.

The cities of Jerusalem and Babylon were not just physical locations. They were pictures of two whole systems of living, which the Bible always describes in contrast with one another. Jerusalem was the city of God, where your life existed to serve God and his greater purposes. Babylon was the city of man, where your life existed to serve yourself and to make yourself known. The Tower of Babel is a picture of the kind of greed and human ambition that underpinned all of Babylonian culture. Babylon was about pride; Jerusalem was about peace—and pride will always be the enemy of peace.

In the Sermon on the Mount, Jesus puts an interesting twist on the image of cities. He says that *we* are a city on a hill. Ancient cities were made out of sun-reflecting limestone, so when you walked in the valleys and looked up, you would see a city gleaming with light. Cities were an image of security, refuge and hope. Jesus said that we are a city on a hill, and those in the valley should recognize us as a hub of hope and refuge.

I was born in Korea, and growing up I always thought it would be kind of cool to have dual citizenship. (Korean citizens have to serve three years in the army, though, so my dad decided to waive that birthright for me.) Dual citizenship is another good picture of our relationship with the world. We're citizens of the world, but we're also citizens of the Kingdom of God. Maybe this seems like a potential conflict of interest, but it shouldn't be. Citizens of the city of God should make the very best citizens of the world. We should be contributing, giving and serving—never using, abusing or exploiting. Far from being at war with the world, we should be the most useful, peaceful, engaged citizens of this world.

When it comes to our future, we can go the way of the Babylonians and blend in to the culture. Or we can go the way of the Jewish leaders and reject the culture. Or we can choose a third way, the way God commanded the Israelites to choose, and seek the peace and prosperity of our communities. We can live this way knowing that God's intentions toward us are good, and that his desire is to bless us and not to harm us. How do we go about that third way? God's instructions to the Israelites can be boiled down to three commissions: engage, influence, and restore.

Engage

God tells the Israelites in verse five, "Build homes and settle down; plant gardens and eat what they produce." In other words: put down roots. Participate. Make a life. Don't live out of your suitcase.

Every Friday night in the community where we lived in Chicago, our neighbors would build bonfires and visit one another. When we first moved in and heard about this tradition, we decided we would keep our Friday nights open so that we could participate. We made a conscious choice that if this was going to be our home, we would invest in it. If these were going to be our neighbors, we would engage them. Not many neighborhoods have that kind of open format for regular interaction, but what would it look like to engage your community? What would it look like to really put down roots and integrate yourself in your neighbor's lives?

Influence

In verse six: "Marry and have sons and daughters; find wives for your sons and give your daughters in marriage, so that they too may have sons and daughters. Increase in number there; do not decrease." When a group gains in numbers, it gains in influence. God was telling the Israelites to make a home for themselves in Babylon, but to stay set apart as a people, and to gain in numbers and influence. He didn't want them to hide out or stay quiet or dissolve into the Babylonian culture. How about you? Would your neighbors describe you as an indistinguishable member of the community, or do they know your identity as a follower of Jesus?

Are you trying to fit in or are you seeking to influence?

Restore

Verse seven: "Also, seek the peace and prosperity of the city to which I have carried you into exile. Pray to the Lord for it, because if it prospers, you too will prosper." This word peace, *shalom*, doesn't simply mean the end of hostility. To pray for shalom in Babylon is to pray that the whole community will flourish and prosper—economically, socially, spiritually, and in every other sense. God was asking his people to pray for the city of God to be established in the city of man, just as Jesus taught us to pray for the Kingdom of God to be established here on earth. To people who had been uprooted from their homes, whose crops had been burned and whose future looked dark and hopeless, God said: Build new homes. Plant new gardens. Have children. Grow in numbers and influence. Engage this city and pray for its restoration.

There was a day when the king rode through the streets of Jerusalem on a donkey while the people shouted *Hosanna*. Just a few days later, this very same king was expelled from the city that had welcomed and praised him. Hebrews 13:12 says, "And so Jesus also suffered outside the city gate, to make the people holy through his own blood." Jesus suffered in a great, cosmic exile so that we could return home. The king was expelled from the city of God so that we could be made permanent citizens of it.

"For I know my plans for you," says the Lord.

Jeremiah 29:11 is a verse for our future. God has plans to prosper and not to harm us. But we have to move into our future His way. Whenever we're asking questions about living life God's way, the underlying question is always, "Can I trust God? Does he really have my best interests at heart?" The sacrifice Jesus made is proof that no matter what darkness and difficulty we face on this earth, God has a hope and a future for his children. Trusting this assurance, let's open our eyes to see life God's way as we engage, influence, and restore the world around us. Does God have a plan for our lives, and is it good? Yes. And he invites us to start living it now.

Life Application

1. When you think of your future, what comes to mind?

2. How do you find yourself blending in too much with society trying to ensure a good future for your life?

3. How do you find yourself hiding out too much from society?

4. What does engaging, influencing and restoring look like for you in your community?

ABOUT THE AUTHOR

Joel Holm is a life-long learner and a strategic thinker who has always wanted to make the world a better place, especially for the weak and the vulnerable. Motivated by his faith, Joel has a passion to help corporations, churches and civic organizations make a genuine, long-lasting impact through creative entrepreneurial initiatives. Joel considers himself to be a child of God and an honest seeker of truth. He has written numerous books, traveled to more than 90 countries, and studied countless models of business, charity and everything in between. From his vast and unique experiences, Joel brings a wealth of insight and learning to every forum in which he speaks and leads. Joel is most grateful that he gets to share his adventurous life with his wife, Marie, and their three children.

To contact Joel and access additional resources visit
Joelholm.com

Made in the USA
San Bernardino, CA
04 May 2015